50
Beaded Earrings

Step-by-Step Techniques for Beautiful Beaded Designs

EDITED BY

Tammy Honaman

penguinrandomhouse.com

1 3 5 7 9 10 8 6 4 2

ISBN-13: 978-1-63250-686-3

EDITORIAL DIRECTOR: Kerry Bogert

EDITOR: Tammy Honaman

CONTENT EDITOR: Nathalie Mornu

EDITORIAL COORDINATOR: Hayley DeBerard

ART DIRECTOR & COVER DESIGNER: Ashlee Wadeson

INTERIOR LAYOUT: Karla Baker

ILLUSTRATOR: Bonnie Brooks

PHOTOGRAPHERS: George Boe, Joe Coca,
Donald Scott, and Ann Swanson

Contents

1 Berry Burst • 4

2 Drops of Rain • 8

3 Quatrefoil • 12

4 Duo Drop • 16

5 Thistle Flower • 20

6 Pergola • 24

7 Fan Flower • 28

8 Enchanted Rivoli • 32

9 Yafa Petal • 36

10 Barcelona Tile • 42

11 Marrakech • 46

12 Heliotrope • 50

13 Blue Jean Queen • 54

14 Floret • 56

15 Floral Swirl • 58

16 Halo • 61

17 Fire & Ice • 64

18 Coachella • 69

19 Dancing Birch • 72

20 Candlelight • 75

21 Crystal Falls • 78

22 Equilateral • 83

23 Retro Blossom • 86

24 Desert Thistle • 88

25 Tundra • 91

26 Season's Delights • 94

27 Parthenope • 97

28 Royal Amethyst • 100

29 Flamenco Flourish • 103

30 Ruby Ripples • 106

31 Sundial • 108

32 Drop-Dead Gorgeous • 112

33 Ice Drop • 115

34 Crystal Cage • 118

35 Swing Time • 120

36 Briolette Bauble • 124

37 Peyote Star • 128

38 Kumi Hoops • 132

39 Incanto • 136

40 Swinging Chevron • 140

41 Waxing Crescent Moon • 144

42 Evening Star • 149

43 Ancient Portals • 152

44 Flower Basket • 156

45 Cathedral Windows • 160

46 Rising Phoenix • 164

47 Four Corners • 170

48 Champagne Serenade • 174

49 Tulip Mania • 177

50 Arabesque • 180

Beading Techniques • 184

Wirework Techniques • 189

Contributors • 191

MAIN COLORWAY.

Berry Burst

Agnieszka Watts

techniques

Circular peyote stitch variation

Picot

Right-angle weave variation

materials

1 g matte light olive over light yellow opaque size 15° Japanese seed beads (A)

0.5 g silver-lined dark peridot frosted size 11° Japanese seed beads (B)

0.5 g silver-lined teal size 8° Japanese seed beads (C)

2 g olive gold marbled opaque 5×2.5mm 2-hole SuperDuos (D)

12 teal luster 6mm 1-hole lentils (E)

6 turquoise 2XAB 3mm crystal bicones (F)

8 fuchsia saturated 4mm fire-polished rounds (G)

4 teal saturated 4mm fire-polished rounds (H)

2 turquoise 5×16mm pressed-glass daggers (J)

2 madder rose halo 8mm pressed-glass melon rounds (K)

1 pair of gold-plated 12×19mm ear wires

Smoke 4 lb FireLine braided beading thread

tools

Scissors

Size 12 beading needle

2 pairs of chain- or flat-nose pliers

FINISHED SIZE: 2¾" (7cm)

1 Earring

Use a variation of circular peyote stitch, picots, and a variation of right-angle weave to form the earring:

ROUND 1: Use 4' (1.2m) of thread to string {1D, 1B, 1D, 1B, 1D, 1C, 1G, and 1C} twice, leaving a 20" (51cm) tail. Pass through the beads (same holes of the D) again to form a tight circle; use the working and tail threads to tie a knot and pass through the first (inside) hole of the first D strung and the nearest 1B/1D (inside hole) (FIG. 1).

CENTER: String 1K and pass through the mirror D (inside hole) of Round 1, then pass back through the K and pass through the last D (inside hole) exited (FIG. 2, BLUE THREAD); repeat the thread path to reinforce. Pass through the nearest 1B/1D (inside hole)/1C (FIG. 2, RED THREAD).

ROUND 2: String 3E; skip the nearest G and pass through the next C, then weave through beads to exit from the third D (inside then outside holes) of the nearest 3D in Round 1 (FIG. 3, GREEN THREAD). String 1D and pass through the nearest D (outside hole) of Round 1; repeat. Pass through the inside hole of the current D and weave through beads to exit from the next C of Round 1 (FIG. 3, BLUE THREAD). Repeat from the beginning of this round (FIG. 3, RED THREAD).

ROUND 3: String 2A, 1F, and 2A; skip the nearest 3E and pass through the next C of Round 1 (FIG. 4, GREEN THREAD). Weave through beads to exit from the nearest D (inside then outside holes) of Round 2 (FIG. 4, BLUE THREAD). String 1G; pass through the nearest D (outside then inside holes) of Round 2 and weave through beads to exit from the next C of Round 1 (FIG. 4, RED THREAD). Repeat from the beginning of this round.

ROUND 4: Weave through beads to exit from the second D (inside hole) of the nearest 2D in Round 2 (FIG. 5, GREEN THREAD). *String 1A, 1H, and 1A; pass through the nearest D (inside hole) of Round 2 (FIG. 5, BLUE THREAD). Weave through beads to exit from the mirror D (inside hole) of Round 2 (FIG. 5, RED THREAD). Repeat from *.

EAR-WIRE LOOP: Weave through beads to exit from the nearest G of Round 3 (FIG. 6, GREEN THREAD). String 7A; pass through the last G exited and the first 5A just added (FIG. 6, BLUE THREAD). String 8A; pass through the last 3A exited (FIG. 6, RED THREAD). Secure this working thread and trim.

FIG. 1: Forming Round 1

FIG. 2: Adding the center

FIG. 3: Working Round 2

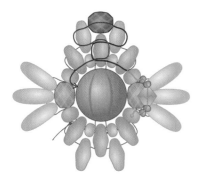

FIG. 4: Starting Round 3

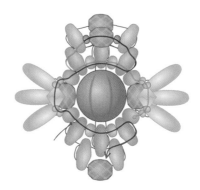

FIG. 5: Beginning Round 4

FIG. 6: Adding the ear-wire loop

DANGLE: Weave the tail thread through beads to exit from the mirror G of Round 3. String 7A; pass through the last G exited and the first 4A just added (FIG. 7, GREEN THREAD). String 1F, 3A, 1J, and 3A; pass back through the F and pass through the last A exited (FIG. 7, BLUE THREAD). Pass through the next 3A/1G (FIG. 7, RED THREAD). Secure the thread and trim.

② Finish

Attach an ear wire to the ear-wire loop by opening and closing the loop of the ear wire as you would a jump ring. *NOTE: Take care to string the ear wire so that the front faces the same direction as the beads of Rounds 3 and 4.*

③ Repeat Steps 1 and 2 for a second earring.

Artist's Tip

- You can string the ear wire while forming the ear-wire loop, instead of adding it later. However, it's probably best to add it later so you can choose the ear wire that looks best with the finished piece.

variations

You can use smooth 8mm rounds or pearls instead of the melon rounds.

Try replacing the 4mm fire-polished rounds with smooth 4mm rounds.

To make a matching pendant, form one earring with a larger bail instead of the ear-wire loop and string a piece of chain, strand of beads, or leather cord instead of an ear wire.

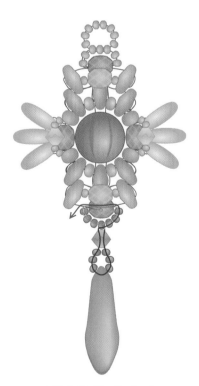

FIG. 7: Stitching the dangle

Drops of Rain

Evelina Palmontová

techniques

Square stitch

Tubular netting

Picot

materials

1 g bright sterling silver–plated size 15° Japanese seed beads (A)

2 g silver galvanized size 11° Japanese seed beads (B)

1 g metallic hematite size 11° Japanese seed beads (C)

1 g matte metallic patina iris 6mm bugle beads (D)

8 turquoise 3mm crystal bicones (E)

2 aquamarine AB 5.5×11mm crystal teardrops

2 foil-back light turquoise 14mm crystal rivolis

8 light cyan 4mm pearl rounds (F)

1 pair of stainless steel 20mm ear wires

Crystal 6 lb FireLine braided beading thread

tools

Scissors

Size 11 beading needle

FINISHED SIZE: 2¾" (7cm)

MAIN COLORWAY

① Bezel

Use square stitch, tubular netting, and picots to bezel the rivoli:

ROUND 1: Use 2½' (76cm) of thread to string {1F, 1B, 1D, and 1B} four times, leaving a 4" (10cm) tail. Pass through the first 1F/1B/1D strung (FIG. 1, BLACK THREAD).

ROUND 2: String 5B and pass through the last D exited to form a square stitch, then weave through beads to exit from the next D of Round 1; repeat three times. Pass through the first 5B of this round (FIG. 1, PURPLE THREAD). *NOTE: You'll now begin working in the opposite direction.*

ROUND 3: String 1B and pass through the nearest 5B of Round 2; repeat three times. Pass through the nearest D of Round 1 (FIG. 1, RED THREAD). *NOTE: You'll now begin working in the opposite direction.*

ROUND 4: String 1D and pass through the last D exited to form a square stitch, then pass through the nearest B of Round 1 (FIG. 2, BLACK THREAD). String 2B, 1E, and 2B; skip the nearest F of Round 1 and pass through the following 1B/1D (FIG. 2, PURPLE THREAD). Repeat from the beginning of this round three times. Weave through beads to exit from the first E of this round (FIG. 2, RED THREAD). Place 1 rivoli faceup into the beadwork so the back of the rivoli touches Rounds 2 and 3.

ROUND 5: While holding the rivoli in place, string 1D and pass through the next E of Round 4; repeat three times (FIG. 3). Repeat the thread path of this round to snug the beads up and over the top of the rivoli.

ROUND 6: Pass through the nearest 2B of Round 4 (FIG. 4, GREEN THREAD). *String 4B; pass up through the mirror 2B of Round 4. String 4B; pass down through the last 2B exited, through the first 4B just added, up through the mirror 2B of Round 4, and through the nearest 1E/2B (FIG. 4, BLUE THREAD). Repeat from * three times. Pass through the nearest 1B/1F of Round 1 (FIG. 4, RED THREAD). *NOTE: You'll now begin working in the opposite direction.*

ROUND 7: String 3C and pass through the nearest D of Round 1 to form a picot, then string 3C and pass through the next F of Round 1; repeat three times. Pass through the next 3C/1D/2C (FIG. 5, BLUE THREAD).

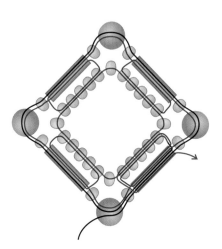

FIG. 1: Stitching Rounds 1–3

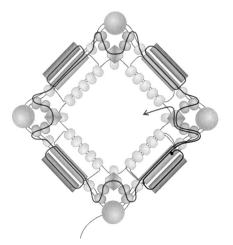

FIG. 2: Working Round 4

FIG. 3: Forming Round 5

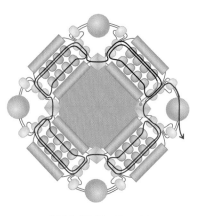

FIG. 4: Stitching Round 6

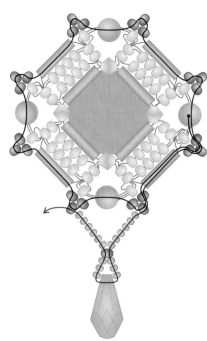

FIG. 5: Adding Round 7 and the dangle

② Dangle

String 6A, 1C, 3A, 1 teardrop, and 3A; pass back through the last C strung. String 6A; pass through the center C of the nearest picot in Round 7 (FIG. 5, RED THREAD). Weave through beads to exit from the center C of the mirror picot in Round 7, at the opposite end of the earring.

③ Ear Wire

String 6A, 1C, 3B, an ear wire, and 3B; pass back through the last C strung. String 6A; pass through the center C of the nearest picot in Round 7 (FIG. 6). *NOTE: Make sure to string the ear wire so that the front of the ear wire faces the same direction as the front of the rivoli. Secure the threads and trim.*

④ Repeat Steps 1–3 for a second earring.

variations

Make a matching pendant by stringing a chain instead of an ear wire.

Use twisted bugle beads instead of the smooth ones shown here.

FIG. 6: Attaching the ear wire

Quatrefoil

Lisa Kan

techniques

Right-angle weave

Square stitch

materials

1 g Montana blue gold luster size 15° Japanese seed beads (A)

1 g bronze size 15° Japanese seed beads (B)

1 g Montana blue gold luster size 11° Japanese seed beads (C)

8 matte gold 4×6mm Czech glass pellet beads (D)

8 fuchsia 3mm crystal bicones (E)

16 dark orange opal 3mm fire-polished rounds (F)

8 cream rose 3mm crystal pearls (G)

8 cream rose 4mm crystal pearls (H)

1 pair of gold-filled 11×18mm ear wires with 3mm ball

Smoke 6 lb FireLine braided beading thread

tools

Scissors

Size 12 beading needle

FINISHED SIZE: 1 1/8 × 1 3/4" (2.9 × 4.5cm)

MAIN COLORWAY

① Body

Use right-angle weave to form the body of the earring:

ROUND 1: Use 5' (1.8m) of thread to string {1D and 1C} four times, leaving a 6" (15cm) tail. Use the working and tail threads to tie a knot, forming a tight circle; pass through the first 1D/1C strung (FIG. 1, GREEN THREAD).

ROUND 2: String 3C; pass through the last C exited and the next D. String 1A, 1C, 1H, 1C, and 1A; pass through the last D exited and the next C (FIG. 1, BLUE THREAD). Repeat from the beginning of this round three times, but do not pass through the next C at the end of the third repeat. Step up through the last 1A/1C/1H/1C added (FIG. 1, RED THREAD).

ROUND 3: String 1C, 1E, and 1C and pass through the nearest 1C/1H/1C of Round 2; repeat three times (FIG. 2).

ROUND 4: String 1F, 1A, and 1F and pass through the nearest 1C/1H/1C of Round 2; repeat three times. Pass through the first 1F/1A added in this round (FIG. 3, BLACK THREAD).

ROUND 5: String 1G, 1B, and 1G; pass through the mirror A of Round 4, back through the 1G/1B/1G just added, through the last A exited in Round 4, and through the first 1G/1B added in this round (FIG. 3, PURPLE THREAD). String 1G; pass through the fourth A of Round 4, back through the G just added, and through the last B exited. String 1G; pass through the second A of Round 4, back through the G just added, and through the last B exited (FIG. 3, GREEN THREAD). Weave through beads to exit from the center C of one 3C set of Round 2 (FIG. 3, RED THREAD).

② Petals

Use square stitch to form petals around the earring body:

ROUND 6: Turn the beadwork over. String 15A and pass through the center C of the next 3C set of Round 2; repeat three times. Pass through the first 2A added in this round (FIG. 4, ORANGE THREAD; back view of beadwork shown).

ROUND 7: String 1B and pass through the last A exited and the next A of Round 6; repeat twelve times. Pass through the next 1C/2A (FIG. 4, PINK THREAD). String 1B and pass through the last A exited and the next A of Round 6; repeat five times. String 3B; pass through the last A exited and the next A of Round 6. String 1B and pass through the last A exited and the next A of Round 6; repeat five times. Pass through the next 1C/2A (FIG. 4, PURPLE THREAD). Repeat from the beginning of this round, passing through only the next 1C/1A at the end of the repeat (FIG. 4, BLUE THREAD).

ROUND 8: Pass through the nearest 13B of Round 7, the next 1A/1C/1A, the following 15B of Round 7, and the next 1A/1C/1A. Repeat from the beginning of this round (FIG. 4, RED THREAD).

③ Loop

Turn the beadwork over. Weave through beads to exit from the eighth B of the nearest 15B set of Round 7. String 6A; pass through the last B exited. Repeat the thread path of the loop to reinforce (FIG. 5). Secure the threads and trim. Attach an ear wire to the loop.

 Repeat Steps 1–3 for a second earring.

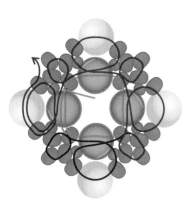

FIG. 1: Stitching Rounds 1 and 2

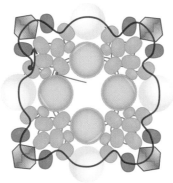

FIG. 2: Working Round 3

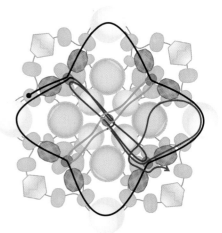

FIG. 3: Adding Rounds 4 and 5

variations

Go with a monochromatic color scheme or one that's nearly monochromatic but punctuated with contrasting metal beads at the outer corners of the center.

FIG. 4: Working Rounds 6–8

FIG. 5: Adding the ear-wire loop

MAIN COLORWAY

Duo Drop

Barbara Falkowitz and Amy Haftkowycz

techniques

Peyote stitch

Picot

Wireworking

materials

1 g sage Picasso size 15° seed beads (A)

1 g metallic mauve size 11° seed beads (B)

2.5 g dark eggplant metallic 5×2.5mm SuperDuos (C)

32 soft jonquil gold opal 2×1.5mm crystal rondelles (D)

6 soft jonquil gold opal 4×3mm crystal rondelles (E)

12 antiqued copper 3×1mm fluted bead caps (F)

2 antiqued copper 14×18mm 1-to-2-hole filigree connectors

1 pair of antiqued copper 11×12mm lever-back ear wires

Smoke 6 lb FireLine braided beading thread

9" (23 cm) of copper half-hard 22-gauge wire

tools

Size 10 beading needle

Wire cutters

Round-nose pliers

2 pairs of chain- or flat-nose pliers

FINISHED SIZE: 2¾" (7cm)

1 Body

Form a wire hoop for the base structure, string beads onto the wire, and then work peyote stitch and picots:

ROW 1: Use one 4½" (11.5cm) piece of wire to form a small (3mm) simple loop. String 3B, 1F (narrow end first), 5D, and 1F (wide end first). String {1C and 1A} nine times. String 1C, 1F (narrow end first), 5D, 1F (wide end first), and 3B; form a simple loop at the other end of the wire. *NOTE: The beads will fit very loosely on the wire; the wire will later be trimmed to resize the loop.* Shape the beaded wire into a round hoop (FIG. 1).

ROW 2: Use 3' (91.5cm) of thread to string 1B; pass through the B again to form a stop bead, leaving an 8" (20.5cm) tail. Pass through the bottom hole of the first C added in Row 1. String 1D; pass through the bottom hole of the next C. String 1C and pass through the bottom hole of the next C; repeat six times. String 1D; pass through the bottom hole of the last C in Row 1 (FIG. 2, GREEN THREAD).

ROW 3: String 1B; pass back through the bottom hole of the last C exited and weave through beads to exit back through the top hole of the first C added in Row 2. String 3A; pass through the bottom hole of the C just exited to form a picot (FIG. 2, BLUE THREAD).

ROW 4: String 1D and pass through the bottom hole of the next C; repeat. String 2C and pass through the bottom hole of the next C; repeat. String 1D and pass through the bottom hole of the next C; repeat. String 3A; pass back through the top hole of the C just exited (FIG. 2, RED THREAD). Weave through beads to exit from the last C added in this row (FIG. 3, GREEN THREAD).

ROW 5: String 3A; pass through the bottom hole of the C just exited. String 1E; pass through the bottom holes of the next 2C. String 1E; pass through the bottom hole of the next C. String 3A; pass through the top hole of the C just exited, the top holes of the next 3C, the 3A previously added, the bottom hole of the last C exited, and the first E added in this row (FIG. 3, BLUE THREAD).

ROW 6: String 1B, 1F (narrow end first), 1E, 1F (wide end first), and 1B; pass back through the second E of Row 5 (FIG. 3, RED THREAD). Secure and trim the working thread; don't trim the tail thread. Untie the stop bead, leaving the bead on the tail thread. Add a needle to the tail thread. Pass through the bottom hole of the first C in Row 1 and the next 4 beads. Secure the thread and trim.

2 Finishing

Slide the beadwork down the wire until it sits next to one of the simple loops. Trim the end of the wire farthest from the beadwork ¼" (6mm) past the end of the beadwork and form a 3mm simple loop. Reshape the hoop as needed. Position the simple loops so that you look at the sides, not through the loops, while the beadwork is flat on your work surface. Opening and closing the simple loops as you would jump rings, attach each simple loop to one bottom hole of the connector. Attach an ear wire to the top hole of the connector.

3 Repeat Steps 1 and 2 for a second earring.

FIG. 1: Stringing Row 1 and forming the hoop

FIG. 2: Working Rows 2–4 of the body

FIG. 3: Stitching Rows 5 and 6 of the body

variations

Connectors come in various styles. Your choice can give the earrings a completely different aesthetic, from Art Nouveau to more contemporary.

Artists' Tips

- Use half-hard wire so the hoops maintain their shape.

- Keep your thread tension loose to prevent buckling the beadwork.

- Before beginning this project, be sure to check that both holes of the SuperDuos are open.

Thistle Flower

Melissa Grakowsky Shippee

techniques

Fringe

Netting

Picot

Right-angle weave

Wireworking

materials

2 g metallic bronze size 15° seed beads (A)

1 g matte metallic blue iris size 15° seed beads (B)

2 g copper-lined matte aqua size 11° seed beads (C)

22 astral pink 3mm crystal bicones (D)

52 white opal AB 4mm crystal bicones (E)

2 matte gray peacock 5×16mm pressed-glass daggers

2 crystal luminous green 12mm crystal rivolis

1 pair of antiqued brass 20×18mm ear wires

Crystal 4 lb braided beading thread

tools

Scissors

Size 12 beading needle

2 pairs of chain- or flat-nose pliers

FINISHED SIZE: 3" (7.5cm)

1 Large Component

Use netting and fringe to form the large component:

ROUND 1: Use 6' (1.8m) of thread to string {1E and 2A} ten times, leaving a 4" (10cm) tail; pass through the first 1E/1A to form a tight circle (FIG. 1, GREEN THREAD).

ROUND 2: String 1B, 1E, 1A, 1B, and 1A; pass back through the last E added and the following B and pass through the following 1A/1E/1A of Round 1 to form a fringe (FIG. 1, BLUE THREAD). Repeat from the beginning of this round nine times. Weave through beads to exit from the B at the tip of the first fringe in this round (FIG. 1, RED THREAD).

ROUND 3: String 1D and pass through the B at the tip of the next 2 fringes in Round 2; repeat four times, pulling tight to cup the beadwork. Pass through the next A (FIG. 2).

ROUND 4: String 1C and pass through the nearest A at the tip of the next Round 2 fringe, arranging the beads so that the C sits underneath the nearest D. Pass through the B at the tip of the next 2 fringes in Round 2 and the following A; repeat four times. Weave through beads to exit from 2A of Round 1 (FIG. 3).

ROUND 5: Turn the beadwork over. String 5A and pass through the next 2A of Round 1; repeat nine times. Step up through the first 3A of this round (FIG. 4).

ROUND 6: Place 1 rivoli faceup into the cupped beadwork. String 2C and pass through the middle A of the next Round 5 net; repeat nine times. Pass through the first 2C of this round (FIG. 5, BLUE THREAD). Pass through the 20C of this round again to secure and tighten the rivoli into place. Weave through beads to exit from the nearest 2A of Round 2 (FIG. 5, RED THREAD).

ROUND 7: String 2A, 1C, and 2A, then pass through the last 2A exited, the next E, and the following 2A; repeat five times. String 5A, then pass through the last 2A exited to form a hanging loop; repeat the thread path to reinforce and pass through the next 1E/2A. String 2A, 1C, and 2A, then pass through the last 2A exited, the next E, and the following 2A; repeat twice. Weave through beads to exit from the first 2A/1C of the loop opposite from the hanging loop (FIG. 6).

FIG. 1: Forming Rounds 1 and 2 of the large component

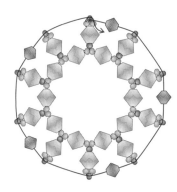

FIG. 2: Stitching Round 3 of the large component

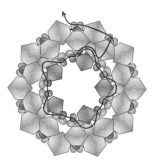

FIG. 3: Adding Round 4 of the large component

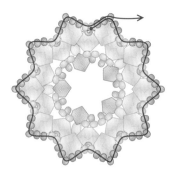

FIG. 4: Working Round 5 of the large component

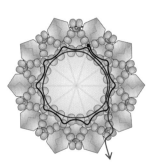

FIG. 5: Stitching Round 6 of the large component

FIG. 6: Working Round 7 of the large component

② Small Component

Use netting, fringe, and picot to form the small component:

CONNECTION LOOP: Use the working thread to string 4A; pass through the last C exited to form a loop. Repeat the thread path to reinforce. Exit from the first 3A just added (FIG. 7, BLUE THREAD).

ROUND 1: String 1E. String {2A and 1E} five times; pass through the second A of the connection loop (FIG. 7, RED THREAD).

ROUND 2: String 1B, 1D, 1A, 1B, and 1A, then pass back through the D just added and the next 1A/1E/1A of the previous round to form a fringe; repeat five times. Step up through the first 1B/1D/1A/1B of this round (FIG. 8, BLUE THREAD).

ROUND 3: Pass through the B at the top of each fringe in Small Component, Round 2 to cup the beadwork; repeat the thread path, then weave through beads to exit from 2A of Small Component, Round 1 (FIG. 8, RED THREAD). *NOTE: Stitch these 6B together so that the beadwork cups in the same direction as the large component, with the D on the same side of the beadwork.*

ROUND 4: Turn the beadwork over. String 5A and pass through the next 2A of Small Component, Round 1; repeat five times, then step up through the first 3A added in this round (FIG. 9, BLUE THREAD).

ROUND 5: String 1C and pass through the middle A of the next 5A net in Small Component, Round 4; repeat five times, pulling tight. Weave through beads to exit from 2A of Small Component, Round 1, opposite from the connection loop (FIG. 9, RED THREAD).

ROUND 6: String 1A, 1C, and 1A, then pass through the last 2A exited and the following 1E/2A; repeat twice. Pass through the following 1E/2A without adding a picot next to the connection loop. String 1A, 1C, and 1A, then pass through the last 2A exited and the following 1E/2A; repeat. Step up through the first 1A/1C of this round (FIG. 10, BLUE THREAD).

DANGLE: String 3A, 1 dagger, and 3A, then pass through the last C exited to form a dangle (FIG. 10, RED THREAD); repeat the thread path to reinforce. Secure the thread and trim.

③ Ear Wire

Attach an ear wire to the topmost loop of the large component by opening and closing the ear wire's loop as you would a jump ring. *NOTE: When attaching the ear wire, keep in mind which side of the earring you'd like to wear in front.*

④ Repeat Steps 1–3 for a second earring.

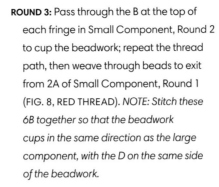

FIG. 7: Forming the connection loop and Round 1 of the small component

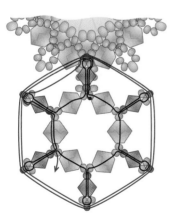

FIG. 8: Stitching Rounds 2 and 3 of the small component

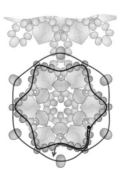

FIG. 9: Adding Rounds 4 and 5 of the small component

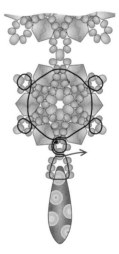

FIG. 10: Forming Round 6 of the small component and adding the dangle

6

Pergola

Penny Dixon

techniques

Circular peyote stitch

Circular netting

Fringe

materials

2 g antiqued pewter size 15º Japanese
  seed beads (A)

10 g antiqued pewter size 11º Japanese
  seed beads (B)

1 g dragonfly blue iris size 8º Japanese
  seed beads (C)

8 orchid 2mm fire-polished rounds (D)

12 polychrome olive-mauve 3mm
  fire-polished rounds (E)

16 polychrome olive-mauve 4mm
  fire-polished rounds (F)

4 purple iris 6mm 4-hole
  QuadraLentils (G)

64 metallic suede dark plum 6×2mm
  2-hole bars (H)

2 medium vitrail 6mm crystal rounds (J)

2 antiqued silver 10×24mm ear wires

Smoke 6 lb FireLine braided beading thread

tools

Scissors

Size 12 beading needle

FINISHED SIZE: 3" (7.5cm)

❶ Circular Base

Use circular peyote stitch to form the base:

BASE ROUNDS 1 AND 2: Use 5' (1.5m) of thread to string {1G, 12B, 1C, 1F, 1C, and 12B} twice, leaving a 2" (5cm) tail. Use the working and tail threads to tie a knot; step up through the first 1G (same hole)/1B strung (FIG. 1, BLUE THREAD). *NOTE: In this and subsequent rounds of the circular base, the thread will always pass through the same (first) hole of each G unless otherwise indicated.*

BASE ROUND 3: Work 6 peyote stitches with 1B in each stitch for a total of 6B; pass through the next F of the previous rounds. String 2F; pass through the last F exited. Work 6 peyote stitches with 1B in each stitch; pass through the next 1G/1B. Repeat from the beginning of this round. Step up through the first B added in this round (FIG. 1, RED THREAD).

BASE ROUND 4: Work 2 peyote stitches with 1B in each stitch. Work 3 peyote stitches with 1C in each stitch. String 1C; pass back through the nearest F of Base Round 3 (FIG. 2, PURPLE THREAD). String 3B; pass back through the next F of Base Round 3. String 2A, 1D, and 2A; pass back through the first F exited in this round. String 2A; pass through the last 1D/2A added and the last F exited (FIG. 2, ORANGE THREAD). Work 4 peyote stitches with 1C in each stitch. Work 2 peyote stitches with 1B in

each stitch; pass through the next 1B/1G (FIG. 2, GREEN THREAD). Pass through the next 4B of Base Rounds 2 and 3; pass back through the nearest B of Round 1, the third B just exited, and the following B of Round 1. String 3B; pass back through the next 3B of Base Rounds 1 and 2. Weave through beads to exit the 2B of Base Rounds 2 and 3 after the nearest G (FIG. 2, BLUE THREAD). Repeat from the beginning of this round. Step up through the bottom-front hole of the nearest G (FIG. 2, RED THREAD).

❷ Diamond

Use netting to form the diamond-shaped structure:

DIAMOND ROUND 1: String {1B and 1H} six times; string 1B and pass through the next F of Base Round 1. String {1B and 1H} six times. String 1B; pass through the next G. *NOTE: In this and subsequent rounds of the diamond, the thread will always pass through the bottom-front hole of the upper G and the top-front hole of the lower G unless otherwise indicated.* Repeat from the beginning of this round. Pass through the first (outside) hole of the first H added in this round, then through the second (inside) hole of the same H (FIG. 3, TURQUOISE THREAD). *NOTE: You will now begin stitching in the opposite direction.*

DIAMOND ROUND 2: String 1A; pass through the next H (inside hole). String 1C; pass through the next H (inside hole). String 1B and pass through the next H (inside hole); repeat twice. *String 1C; pass through the next H (inside hole). String 1A; pass through the next H (inside hole), back through the last C added, and through the next H (inside hole). String 1B and pass through the next H; repeat twice.** Repeat from * to ** twice. Pass back through the nearest C and through the next 1H (inside hole)/1A; weave through beads to exit from the bottom-front hole of the upper G (FIG. 3, RED THREAD).

❸ Top Embellishment

Use circular netting to add a top embellishment that will anchor the ear wire:

TOP EMBELLISHMENT ROUND 1: String 2A; pass through the top-front hole of the current G. String 2A; pass through the bottom-front hole of the G, the 2A just added, and the top-front hole of the G (FIG. 4, PURPLE THREAD). String 1A, 1B, 1D, 1B, and 1A; pass through the top-front hole of the G and the nearest A (FIG. 4, GREEN THREAD). *NOTE: In all remaining rounds of the top embellishment, the thread will always pass through the top-front hole of the upper G.*

FIG. 1: Stitching Base Rounds 1–3

FIG. 2: Working Base Round 4

FIG. 3: Adding the diamond

TOP EMBELLISHMENT ROUND 2: String 1B, 1H, 1A, and 1H; pass through the D of the previous round. String 1H, 1A, 1H, and 1B; pass through the nearest 1A/1G/1A/1B/1H (first/inside hole)/1A/1H (inside hole) (FIG. 4, TURQUOISE THREAD).

TOP EMBELLISHMENT ROUND 3: String 1A, 1B, and 1A; pass through the next 1H (inside hole)/1A/1H (inside hole). String 3A; pass through the second (outside) hole of the current H. String 1E; pass through the next H (outside hole). String 1F; pass through the next H (outside hole). String 1E; pass through the next H (outside hole). String 3A; pass through the inside hole of the current H. Weave through beads to exit from the inside hole of the last H added in Top Embellishment Round 2, the adjacent 3A, and the outside hole of the current H (FIG. 4, RED THREAD).

TOP EMBELLISHMENT ATTACHMENT: Turn the beadwork over. String 1B; pass through the next 1H (outside hole)/1F/1H (outside hole). String 1B; pass through the next 1H (outside hole) and the nearest 1A of Top Embellishment Round 3, then pass back through the last H (outside hole) exited. Weave through beads to exit back through the first B added in this attachment (FIG. 5, BLUE THREAD; back view of beadwork shown). *NOTE: In this attachment, the holes in the G that face you are referred to as the front for instructional purposes, even though you're actually viewing the back of the base.*

String 4A; pass through the top-front hole of the G. String 4A; pass back through the second B added in this attachment. String 5A; pass back through the first B added in this attachment (FIG. 5, RED THREAD). Repeat the entire thread path of this attachment. Weave through beads to exit from the top-front hole of the bottom G.

4 Bottom Embellishment

Use circular netting and fringe to add a bottom arch and decorative fringe:

BOTTOM EMBELLISHMENT ROUNDS 1–3: Rotate the beadwork so that the current G and the working thread are at the top. Repeat Top Embellishment Rounds 1–3. Rotate the beadwork so that the G and the working thread are at the bottom. *NOTE: In this attachment, the holes in the G that face you are referred to as the front for instructional purposes, even though you're actually viewing the back of the base.*

BOTTOM EMBELLISHMENT FRINGE: Pass through the nearest 1E/1H (outside hole). String 3A, 1B, 1J, and 1B; pass back through the last 1J/1B added. String 3A; skip the nearest F and pass through the next 1H (outside hole)/1E/1H (outside hole)/1A. String 1E and 1A; pass through the bottom-front hole of the nearest G. String 1A and 1E; pass through the next A and the first H (outside hole) exited in this fringe (FIG. 6, back view of beadwork shown). Repeat the thread path of this fringe to reinforce. Secure the threads and trim.

5 Ear Wire

Attach an ear wire to the 5A strand added in the top embellishment attachment by opening and closing the ear wire's loop as you would a jump ring.

6 Repeat Steps 1–5 for a second earring.

Artist's Tip

- Use medium tension when stitching the circular base and tight tension when stitching the diamond.

FIG. 4: Working top embellishment Rounds 1–3

FIG. 5: Completing the top embellishment attachment

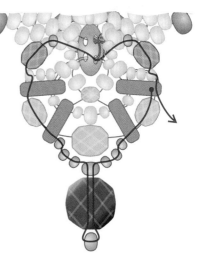

FIG. 6: Adding the bottom embellishment fringe

Fan Flower

Penny Dixon

technique

Netting

Picot

materials

1 g gold luster dark topaz size 15° seed beads (A)

1 g higher metallic amethyst size 11° seed beads (B)

1 g metallic rainbow violet/gold size 11° cylinder beads (C)

1 g gold AB 3.4mm Japanese drops (D)

2 purple gold iris 3mm pressed-glass rounds (E)

4 opaque green luster 3mm fire-polished rounds (F)

4 opaque green luster 4mm fire-polished rounds (G)

2 opaque green luster 6mm fire-polished rounds (H)

22 pink crystal luster 5×16mm 2-hole daggers (I)

2 twilight peridot 6mm flat 2-hole squares (J)

2 opaque green luster 12×16mm pressed-glass
pear-shaped drops (K)

1 pair of gold-filled 17mm ear wires

Smoke 6 lb braided beading thread

tools

Scissors

Size 13 beading needle

FINISHED SIZE: 1¼ × 2¼" (3.2 × 5.5cm)

MAIN COLORWAY

① Circular Base

Use netting and picot stitches to form the earring:

ROUND 1: Use 2' (61cm) of thread to string 1J and 1I (top hole), leaving a 4" (10cm) tail; pass through the bottom hole of the I just strung. String 1I (top hole); pass through the bottom hole of the J just strung (FIG. 1, BLUE THREAD). String 1I (top hole) and 1I (bottom hole); pass through the top hole of the last I strung. Use the working and tail threads to tie a knot and form a tight circle, then pass through the J (top hole) and first I (top hole) of this round (FIG. 1, RED THREAD).

ROUND 2: String 1I (bottom hole), 1A, and 1C; pass through the top hole of the I just strung (FIG. 2, BLUE THREAD). String 1H, 1I (top hole), 1C, and 1A; pass through the bottom hole of the I just added, through the nearest I of Round 1 (top hole), the J (top hole), the first I added in Round 1 (top hole), and through the first I (bottom hole), A, and C added in this round (FIG. 2, RED THREAD).

ROUND 3: String 1B, 1G, 1E, 1G, and 1B; pass through the next 1C/1A of Round 2 and the 3I (bottom holes) along the right side of the earring. String 1B, 1K, and 1B; pass through the next 3I (bottom holes) along the left side of the earring. Weave through the next 1A/1C of Round 2 and the first B added in this round (FIG. 3). Secure and trim the tail thread.

ROUND 4: String 3A and 1F; pass through the E of Round 3. String 1F and 3A; pass through the next 1B/1C/1A/1I (bottom hole)/1I (top hole). String 1I (bottom hole), 1I (top hole), and 1I (bottom hole); pass through first I of Round 1 (top hole), the I added in Round 2 (bottom hole), the following A and C, and the top hole of the last I exited (FIG. 4).

ROUND 5: String 1D and pass through the next I (top hole); repeat twice. Weave through the following 1B/3A/1F. String 3D; pass thread through the next 1F/3A/1B (FIG. 5). *NOTE: This forms the front of the earring.*

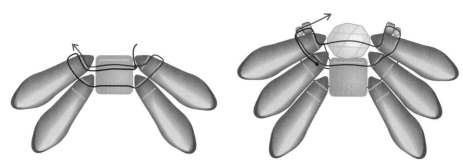

FIG. 1: Forming Round 1

FIG. 2: Adding Round 2

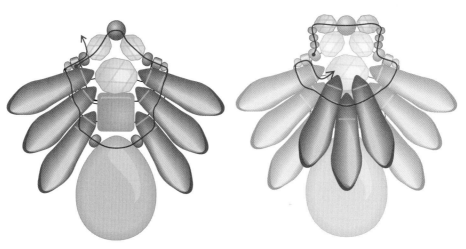

FIG. 3: Stitching Round 3

FIG. 4: Completing Round 4

ROUND 6: Turn the earring over so that the back faces up. Pass through the next 2I (top holes). String 1B, 2I (top holes), and 1B; pass through the next I (top hole), the following I (bottom hole), and the nearest A and C. Pass through top hole of the last I exited and the H (FIG. 6).

ROUND 7: Turn the earring over so that the front is faceup. String 5A; pass down through the G on the left and the following B, I (top hole), and H (FIG. 7, BLUE THREAD). String 3A; pass up through the last 2A added and down through the G on the right and the following B. Weave through beads as shown to exit from the top D added in Round 5 (FIG. 7, RED THREAD).

HANGING LOOP: String 7A; pass through the D just exited to form a loop. Repeat the thread path to reinforce (FIG. 8). Secure the thread and trim. Attach an ear wire to the loop just formed.

2 Repeat to form the second earring.

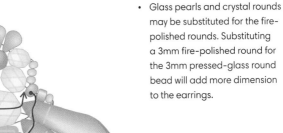

Artist's Tip

- Glass pearls and crystal rounds may be substituted for the fire-polished rounds. Substituting a 3mm fire-polished round for the 3mm pressed-glass round bead will add more dimension to the earrings.

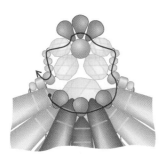

FIG. 5: Forming Round 5

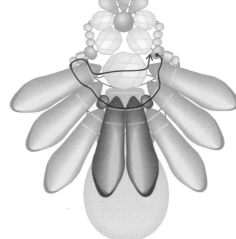

FIG. 6: Stitching Round 6

FIG. 7: Adding Round 7

FIG. 8: Forming the hanging loop

MAIN COLORWAY

Enchanted Rivoli

Csilla Csirmaz

techniques

Tubular peyote stitch

Ladder stitch

Tubular herringbone stitch

Square stitch

materials

2 g bronze size 15° seed beads (A)

2 g bronze size 11° seed beads (B)

2 g bronze size 11° cylinder beads (C)

2 g matte gold luster size 9° seed beads (D)

2 g bronze size 8° seed beads (E)

8 bronze size 6° seed beads (F)

4 fuchsia AB 3mm crystal bicones (G)

20 fuchsia AB2X 4mm crystal bicones (H)

2 amethyst 6mm crystal bicones (I)

2 foil-backed amethyst 12mm crystal rivolis

1 pair of brass ¾" (2cm) ear wires

Smoke 4 lb braided beading thread

tools

Scissors

Size 12 beading needle

FINISHED SIZE: 1⅝" (4.1cm)

❶ Bezel

Work tubular peyote stitch to form a bezel for the rivoli:

ROUNDS 1 AND 2: Use 3' (91.5cm) of thread to string 30A, leaving a 6" (15cm) tail. Tie the working and tail threads together to form a tight knot; pass through the first A strung.

ROUND 3: String 1C, skip 1A, and pass through the next A; repeat fourteen times for a total of 15C. Step up for the next and subsequent rounds by passing through the first bead added in the current round.

ROUNDS 4 AND 5: Work 1C in each stitch for a total of 15C in each of 2 rounds. Set 1 rivoli in the beadwork so the back touches Round 1.

ROUNDS 6 AND 7: Work 1A in each stitch for a total of 15A in each of 2 rounds (FIG. 1), pulling the thread tight to secure the rivoli in place. Secure the threads and trim. Set the bezel aside.

❷ Rope

Work a tubular herringbone-stitched rope to wrap around the bezel:

ROUND 1: Use 6' (91.5 cm) of thread to ladder-stitch a strip 4A long. Stitch the first and last A together to form a ring (FIG. 2).

ROUND 2: String 2A, pass down through the next A of Round 1, and up through the following A; repeat. Step up for the next and subsequent rounds by passing through the first bead added in the current round (FIG. 3).

ROUNDS 3-8: Work 2A in each stitch for a total of 4A. Repeat five times for a total of 6 more rounds.

ROUND 9: Work 2B in each stitch for a total of 4B.

ROUNDS 10-15: Work 2D in the first stitch and 2E in the second stitch (FIG. 4); repeat five times for a total of 6 more rounds.

ROUNDS 16 AND 17: Work 2E in the first stitch and 2F in the second stitch; repeat once for a total of 2 more rounds.

ROUNDS 18-23: Work 2D in the first stitch and 2E in the second stitch; repeat five times for a total of 6 more rounds.

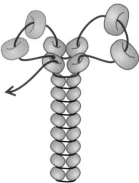

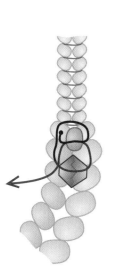

FIG. 1: Forming the bezel

FIG. 2: Connecting Round 1 of the rope

FIG. 3: Stitching Round 2

FIG. 4: Adding Round 10 of the rope

FIG. 5: Embellishing the rope

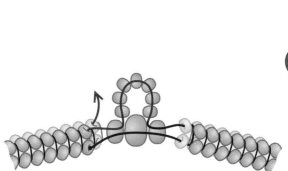

FIG. 6: Connecting the rope ends and adding the loop

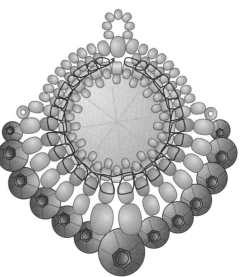

FIG.7: Connecting the bezel to the rope (back view)

ROUND 24: Work 2B in each stitch for a total of 4B.

ROUNDS 25–32: Work 2A in each stitch for a total of 4A; repeat seven times for a total of 8 more rounds. Work a ladder-stitch thread path on the final round to close the end. Weave through beads to exit down through a B in Round 24 that sits above an E in Round 23.

3 Embellish

String 1B; pass up through the next B in Round 24 that sits above an E in Round 23, then pass down through the original B exited and the nearest E in Round 23 (FIG. 5, BLUE THREAD). Working on the same side of the rope where the last embellishment was made, string 1G; pass up through the next E in Round 23, down through the original E exited in this stitch, and the nearest E in Round 22 (FIG. 5, RED THREAD). Using the same technique, continue adding bead embellishments along the edge of the rope in this order: 5H, 1I, 5H, 1G, and 1B. Weave through beads to exit from Round 1 of the rope.

4 Assembly

Connect the rope ends to form a circle, add a hanging loop, and stitch the bezel to the center:

ROPE ENDS: Use the working thread of the rope to string 1B, 1E, and 1B; pass down through 1A on the other end of the rope and up through the adjacent A and the nearest B just added (FIG. 6, BLUE THREAD).

LOOP: String 7A; pass through the first B added in this step, down through the next A at the end of the rope, and up through the adjacent A (FIG. 6, RED THREAD).

REINFORCE: Repeat the thread path of the rope-end connection and the loop several times, taking care to pass through each A at each end of the rope to seat the new beads at the center of the rope ends. Exit from 1A of Round 1, toward the inside of the circle.

BEZEL: Place the bezel in the center of the rope circle. Use a square-stitch thread path to secure the inside of the rope circle to Rounds 3 and 4 of the bezel (FIG. 7). *NOTE: It may be tricky to get the needle between the rope and bezel; just do your best to secure the bezel while keeping the stitches neat. It's fine to pass through 2 beads at a time here; just make sure the bezel is snug.*

Add an ear wire to the loop.

5 Repeat Steps 1–4 for a second earring.

Artist's Tips

- You may use larger rivolis in this earring. Just adjust the bead count in Rounds 1 and 2 of the bezel and be sure to stitch a longer herringbone rope.

- For an extra glamorous pair of earrings, stitch two or even three of these earring components together.

- If you have trouble finding size 9° seed beads, look for a tube or hank of inconsistently sized 8°s and use the smallest beads in place of the 9°s.

BACK OF EARRING

MAIN COLORWAY

Yafa Petal

Penny Dixon

techniques

Square stitch

Odd-count flat peyote stitch

Loop fringe

Picot

Tubular brick stitch

Netting

materials

2 g silver-lined matte peach AB size 15°
Japanese seed beads (A)

2 g bronze size 15° Japanese seed beads (B)

1 g gold-frosted red size 11° Japanese seed
beads (C)

1 g opaque metallic luster rainbow rose
size 11° Japanese cylinder beads (D)

1 g bronze size 8° Japanese seed beads (E)

8 matte purple iris 3mm fire-polished rounds (F)

2 Siam 4mm crystal bicones (G)

2 light Colorado topaz AB 4mm crystal
bicones (H)

2 Siam 6mm crystal rounds (I)

36 transparent red 8×7mm Czech pressed-
glass rose petals (J)

1 pair of gold-plated ⅞" (2.2cm) ear wires

Smoke 6 lb braided beading thread

tools

Scissors

Size 12 beading needle

FINISHED SIZE: 1 ½ × 2 ½" (3.8 × 6.5cm)

① Bezel

Use square stitch, netting, and picots to bezel a crystal round:

BASE BOTTOM: Use 3' (91.5cm) of thread to string 1I and 10A, leaving a 4" (10cm) tail; pass through the 1I (FIG. 1, GREEN THREAD). String 10A; pass through the 1I again, allowing the beads to sit on the other side of the I (FIG. 1, BLUE THREAD). Pass through all 20A plus the first A of the second set again, pulling tight (FIG. 1, RED THREAD).

BASE TOP: String 2A; pass through the last 2A exited and the next 2A of the first bezel round to form a square stitch; repeat nine times to add 20A. Exit the first 2A added in this round (FIG. 2, BLUE THREAD). Weave through beads to exit between the first 2A added in this round (FIG. 2, RED THREAD). Pull the thread tight so the base rounds sit parallel to each other against the crystal (FIG. 3). Pass through the I, exiting between the rounds. Loop around the threads between beads and pass back through the I and through the next 3A of the bottom base round (FIG. 4, PURPLE THREAD).

ROUND 1, RIGHT SIDE: String 2D; pass through the last 2A exited and the next 3A of the bottom base round. String 1F, 1D, and 1F; pass through the last 2A exited and the next A (FIG. 4, GREEN THREAD). String 6B; pass through the nearest D. String 6B; pass through the A just before the last F added (FIG. 4, BLUE THREAD). Weave up through the nearest 1F/1B/1D/1B, down through the next 1F, and through the next 3A of the bottom base round (FIG. 4, RED THREAD).

ROUND 1, BOTTOM: String 2D and pass through the last 2A exited and the next 2A of the bottom base round; repeat twice. Pass through the next 1A of the bottom base round (FIG. 5).

ROUND 1, LEFT SIDE: String 1F, 1D, and 1F; pass through the last 2A exited and the next A of the bottom base round. String 6B; pass through the nearest D. String 6B; pass through the A just before the last F added. Weave up through the nearest 1F/1B/1D/1B, down through the next 1F, and through the next 3A of the bottom base round. String 2D; pass through the last 2A exited and the next 1A of the bottom base round (FIG. 6, BLUE THREAD). *NOTE: This side should mirror the right side.*

FIG. 1: Forming the base bottom

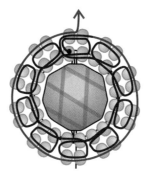

FIG. 2: Adding the base top

FIG. 3: Tightening the base

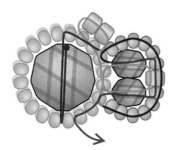

FIG. 4: Stitching the right side of Round 1

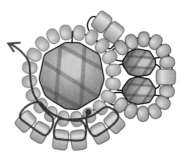

FIG. 5: Adding the bottom of Round 1

ROUND 1, TOP: String 1G and 1D; pass back through the G, the next 3A of the bottom base round, and the first 2D added in Round 1 (FIG. 6, RED THREAD).

ROUND 2, TOP: String 1A; pass through the last 1D exited and the A just added. String 2A; pass through the last 2D exited (FIG. 7, GREEN THREAD). String 2A; pass through the 1D above the bicone. String 5B; pass through the last D exited, forming a loop. String 2A; pass through the nearest 2D of Round 1 (FIG. 7, BLUE THREAD). String 3A; pass through the first of the last 2D exited, the third A just added, the last 2D exited, and the nearest 5B of Round 1 (FIG. 7, RED THREAD).

ROUND 2, SIDES AND BOTTOM: String 3A, 1B, and 3A; skip the nearest 1B/1D/1B of Round 1 and pass through the next 5B and the nearest D. String 1B; pass through the last D exited and the next 5D. String 1B; pass through the last D exited and the nearest 5B of Round 1. String 3A, 1B, and 3A; skip the nearest 1B/1D/1B of Round 1 and pass through the next 4B of Round 1 and the nearest 2A of Round 2 (FIG. 8).

ROUND 3: String 1B; pass through the last A exited, then weave through beads to exit from the second A of the 3A set added in Round 2. String 1B; pass through the last A exited, then weave through beads to exit from 1B at the left side of Round 2. String 3B; pass through the last B exited, then weave through beads to exit from the bottom-right square-stitched B of Round 2, toward the center of the work. String 1D, 1B, 1H, 1B, and 1D; pass through the bottom-left square-stitched B of Round 2 and the last 6D exited and weave through beads to exit from 1B at the right side of Round 2. String 3B; pass through the last B exited, the next 3A of Round 2, and the next 4B of Round 1 (FIG. 9). Secure the thread and trim. Set the bezel aside.

Artist's Tips

- Keep the tension tight when forming the bezel base in Step 1, but avoid knots. Making a knot anywhere will prevent the rounds from lying smoothly against the crystal.

- When square-stitching the cylinder beads on the bezel, pull the thread parallel to the cylinder beads to avoid tearing the thread.

- It might become difficult to pull the needle through the peyote-stitched tube when forming the petal fringe. Use bent-nose pliers to help ease the needle through the beads.

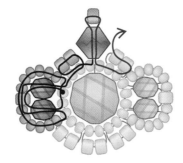

FIG. 6: Forming the top of Round 1

FIG. 7: Stitching the top of Round 2

FIG. 8: Adding the sides and bottom of Round 2

FIG. 9: Forming Round 3

② Fringe Base

Use odd-count flat peyote stitch to form a curved base:

ROWS 1 AND 2: Use 4' (1.2 m) of thread to string {1C and 1D} ten times. String 1C, leaving a 12" (30.5 cm) tail.

ROW 3: Work 10 stitches with 1C in each stitch. String 1C; tie a square knot with the tail and working threads and pass back through the C just added.

ROW 4: Work 10 stitches with 1A in each stitch.

ROW 5: Work 11 stitches with 1A in each stitch. Form an odd-count turnaround at the end of this and the following odd-numbered rows by looping the thread between edge beads of the 2 previous rows and stepping up for the next row by passing back through the last bead added.

ROWS 6-8: Repeat Rows 4 and 5; then repeat Row 4.

ROW 9: Work 11 stitches with 1C in each stitch.

ROW 10: Work 10 stitches with 1D in each stitch.

ROW 11: Repeat Row 9.

ROW 12: Work 10 stitches with 1E in each stitch.

ZIP: Pinch Rows 1 and 12 together so the beads interlock like a zipper. Pass through the final C of Row 1 (FIG. 10). Continue weaving Rows 1 and 12 together, forming a seamless tube. Weave through beads to exit from the second C of Row 3, toward the center.

③ Fringe

Embellish the fringe base with looped fringe:

LOOP 1: String 5B, 1J (from the front side), and 2B; pass through the final E of Row 12 and weave through beads to exit from the next D of Row 2 (FIG. 11).

LOOP 2: String 5B, 1J (from the front side), and 2B; pass through the next C of Row 1 and weave through beads to exit from the next C of Row 3 (FIG. 12). *NOTE: Make sure each new loop is positioned on top of the previous loop.*

LOOPS 3-9: Repeat Loops 1 and 2 three times, then repeat Loop 1, progressing down the fringe base in the same manner. Weave through beads to exit from the sixth C of Row 3, toward the loops already formed.

LOOP 10: The loops will now change direction so they mirror Loops 1-9. String 5B, 1J (from the front side), and 2B; pass through the sixth E of Row 12, forming a loop. Weave through beads to exit from the next C of Row 1 (FIG. 13). *NOTE: The loop will loop over Loop 9.*

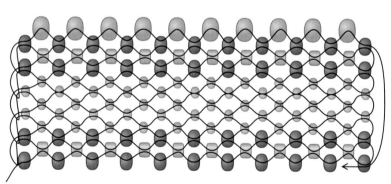

FIG. 10: Working the fringe base

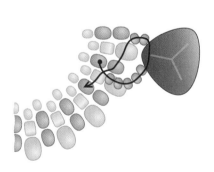

FIG. 11: Adding the first fringe loop

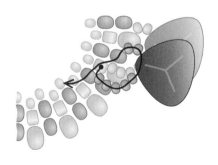

FIG. 12: Working the second fringe loop

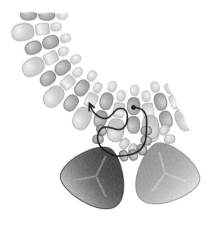

FIG. 13: Forming Loop 10

LOOP 11: String 2B, 1J (from the back side), and 5B; pass through the next D of Row 2 and weave through beads to exit from the next E of Row 12 (FIG. 14).

LOOP 12: String 2B, 1J (from the back side), and 5B; pass through the next C of Row 3 and weave through beads to exit from the following C of Row 1 (FIG. 15).

LOOPS 13–18: Repeat Loops 11 and 12 three times. Weave through beads to exit from the final C of Row 1.

④ Assembly

Connect the fringe base to the bezel:

END: String 2B; pass under the thread loop between end beads of the base and pass back through the second B just added. String 1B; pass under the next thread loop and pass back through the B just added. Continue working tubular brick stitch for a total of 6B, then pass down through the first B added and up through the final B to connect the round (FIG. 16).

LOOP: String 1E and 7B; pass through the loop on the left side of the bezel, back through the E just added, down through 1B on the opposite side of the last brick-stitched round exited, into the fringe base, and up through the next 1B of the brick-stitched round (FIG. 17). *NOTE: Make sure that the fronts of both components face the same direction.* Repeat the thread path to reinforce, working around the brick-stitched round to center the loop. Secure the working thread and trim.

Weave the tail thread through beads to repeat this entire step on the other end of the fringe base, connecting to the right side of the bezel. Attach an ear wire to the loop at the top of the bezel.

⑤ Repeat Steps 1–4 for a second earring.

FIG. 14: Adding Loop 11

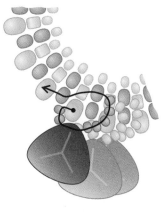

FIG. 15: Stitching Loop 12

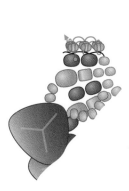

FIG. 16: Brick-stitching the fringe-base end

FIG. 17: Connecting the fringe base and bezel

Barcelona Tile

Maggie Meister

techniques

Circular peyote stitch

Square stitch

materials

1 g gold size 15° seed beads (A)

5 g silver-lined blue size 15° seed beads (B)

7 g metallic gold size 11° cylinder beads (C)

5 g metallic blue iris size 11° cylinder beads (D)

5 g matte terra cotta size 11° cylinder beads (E)

10 lapis lazuli 2mm rounds

2 lapis lazuli 10×10mm flat briolettes

1 pair of silver earring posts with 10mm pads and
    ear nuts

Gold size D nylon beading thread

Double-sided craft tape

tools

Scissors

Size 10 or 12 English beading needle

Size 12 sharp beading needle

FINISHED SIZE: 2½" (6.5cm)

❶ Component

Use circular peyote stitch to form a double-sided component:

ROUND 1: Use 3' (91.5cm) of thread to string 6C, leaving a 4" (10cm) tail. Pass through the beads again to form a tight circle. Pass through the first bead (FIG. 1, BLUE THREAD).

CENTER: String 1A, one 2mm round, and 1A; pass through 1C on the other side of Round 1, then pass back through the 1A/round/1A just strung and through the last C exited on the other side of Round 1 (FIG. 1, RED THREAD).

ROUND 2: String 1C and pass through the next C of Round 1; repeat five times for a total of 6C. Step up through the first C added in this round (FIG. 2, GREEN THREAD).

ROUND 3: Work 6 stitches with 1D in each stitch. Step up through the first D added in this round (FIG. 2, BLUE THREAD).

ROUND 4: Work 6 stitches with 2E in each stitch. Step up through the first 2E added in this round (FIG. 2, RED THREAD).

ROUND 5: Work 6 stitches with 1E in each stitch, treating the 2E sets added in the previous round as 1 bead. Step up through the first E added in this round (FIG. 3, GREEN THREAD).

ROUND 6: Work 6 stitches with 3C in each stitch. Step up through the first 3C added in this round (FIG. 3, BLUE THREAD).

ROUND 7: Work 6 stitches with 2C in each stitch, treating the 3C sets added in the previous round as 1 bead (FIG. 3, RED THREAD).

ROUND 8: String 1C and pass through the next 3C of Round 6; repeat five times. Step up through the first C added in this round (FIG. 4, ORANGE THREAD). *NOTE: You'll now be forming the back of the component.*

ROUND 9: Work 6 stitches with 2C in each stitch. Step up through the first 2C added in this round (FIG. 4, GREEN THREAD).

ROUND 10: Work 6 stitches with 1C in each stitch, treating the 2C sets added in the previous round as 1 bead. Step up through the first C added in this round (FIG. 4, BLUE THREAD).

ROUND 11: Work 6 stitches with 1C in each stitch. Step up through the first C added in this round (FIG. 4, RED THREAD).

FIG. 1: Forming Round 1 and the center embellishment of the component

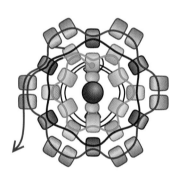

FIG. 2: Adding Rounds 2–4 of the component

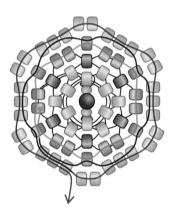

FIG. 3: Stitching Rounds 5–7 of the component

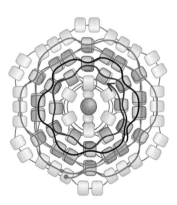

FIG. 4: Adding Rounds 8–11 of the component

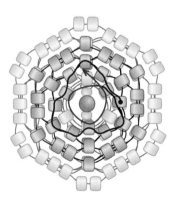

FIG. 5: Stitching Round 12 of the component

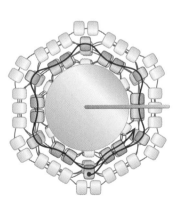

FIG. 6: Adding the earring post

ROUND 12: String 1C and pass through the next C of Round 11, the nearest C of Round 10, and the following C of Round 11; repeat twice for a total of 3C. Step up through the first C added in this round (FIG. 5, BLUE THREAD). Pass through the 3C just added to tighten the center (FIG. 5, RED THREAD). Secure the thread and trim. Set the component aside.

Repeat this entire step for a second terra-cotta–colored component. Repeat this entire step twice more, substituting D for E and E for D, to form 2 blue components.

② Post Component

Use 5′ (1.6 m) of thread to repeat Step 1 to form a terra-cotta component, but after completing Round 9, place a small piece of double-sided tape on the front of 1 earring pad and adhere it to the beadwork as shown (FIG. 6). Continue working Rounds 10–12, firmly securing the earring finding within the beadwork. Exit from 2C at the edge of the component (Round 7). Don't trim the thread.

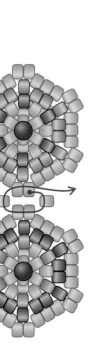

FIG. 7: Connecting the post component to a blue component

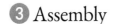

③ Assembly

Use square stitch to connect Round 7 of the components:

POST: Use the working thread on the post to string 1C; pass through 2C at the corner edge of 1 blue component, vertically aligning each 1A/round/1A center embellishment. String 1C; pass through the last 2C exited on the post component to connect (FIG. 7).

BODY: Arrange the components as shown in FIG. 0, vertically aligning each 1A/round/1A center embellishment. Weave the working thread through beads to square-stitch 1C to 1C at the points indicated, completely connecting the components and repeating each connection to secure.

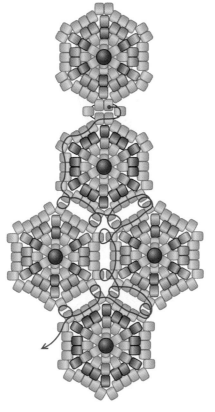

FIG. 8: Assembling the body of the earring

BRIOLETTE: Weave through beads to exit from 2C at the bottom point of the bottom component. String 2C, 1 briolette, and 2C, then pass through the last 2C exited from the component to form a loop; repeat the thread path to reinforce and exit from 1C of the bottom point (FIG. 9, BLUE THREAD).

EDGE: String 1B; pass through the next C at the bottom point. *Weave through beads to exit from the first of the next 2C at the edge of the component. String 1B; pass through the next C at the edge. Repeat from * around the entire edge of the earring to embellish the edge (FIG. 9, RED THREAD). Secure the thread and trim.

④ Repeat Steps 1–3 for a second earring.

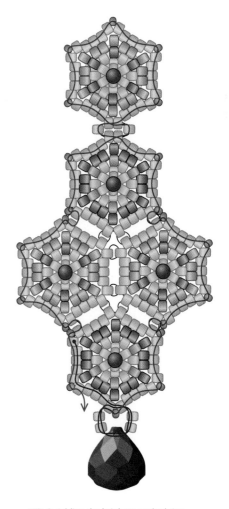

FIG. 9: Adding the briolette and edging

Marrakech

Lisa Kan

techniques
Peyote stitch
Herringbone stitch
Picot
Netting

materials
2 g green teal luster size 15° seed beads (A)
3 g chartreuse luster size 15° seed beads (B)
2 g gunmetal size 15° cylinder beads (C)
2 g metallic green iris 1.5mm cube beads (D)
8 blue zircon 3mm crystal bicones
2 metallic sage 3×4mm potato pearls
1 pair of gold-filled ear wires with 3mm ball
Smoke 6 lb braided beading thread

tools
Size 12 beading needles
Scissors
Chain- or flat-nose pliers

FINISHED SIZE: 1¾" (4.5cm)

① Top Connector

Use 18" (45.5 cm) of thread and a combination of herringbone and netting stitches to work a triangle that will serve as the connector for the ear wire:

ROUND 1: String 6C, leaving a 5" (12.5cm) tail. Pass through the first bead strung to form a circle. Keep the circle tight by holding the beadwork between the thumb and index finger of your nondominant hand while you are working.

ROUND 2: String 2C and pass through the next 2C of Round 1; repeat around to add a total of 6C. Step up for the next round by passing through the first bead added in this round (FIG. 1).

ROUND 3: String 2C; pass through the next 1C of Round 2. String 1D, skip 2C of Round 1, and pass through the next 1C of Round 2. Repeat around to add a total of 6C and 3D. Step up for the next round by passing through the first bead added in this round (FIG. 2).

ROUND 4: String 1A; pass through the next 1C of Round 3. String 7B; skip the 1D from Round 3 and pass through the following 1C of Round 3. Repeat around to add a total of 3A and 21B. Step up for the next round by passing through the fourth B added in this round (FIG. 3).

CONNECTING ROUND: Pass through the fourth B in the next 7B net of Round 4; repeat to connect the third net, forming a three-dimensional triangle (FIG. 4). Repeat the thread path to reinforce; secure the thread and trim. Set the connector aside.

② Basket

Using the same general triangle pattern as in Step 1, work a series of conjoined triangles in a basket shape:

TRIANGLE 1: Repeat Step 1 to form a triangle but use 7A (instead of 7B) for one of the nets in Round 4. Set aside.

TRIANGLE 2: Repeat Step 1, Rounds 1 and 2. Repeat Step 1, Round 3, but instead of adding a third D, stitch into the side D of Triangle 1, positioning Triangle 1 so its net made with A beads is at the bottom (FIG. 5). Repeat Step 1, Round 4, but use 7A for the bottom right net. Repeat the Step 1 connecting round and exit the top of the triangle, between this triangle and Triangle 1. String 1 bicone; pass through the connecting round of Triangle 1, back through the crystal, and into the connecting round of this triangle (FIG. 6). Secure the thread and trim. Set aside.

TRIANGLE 3: Repeat Triangle 2, connecting to the right-side D of the previous triangle and adding 1 bicone between Triangles 2 and 3.

TRIANGLE 4: Repeat Triangle 2, this time starting with 30" (76 cm) of thread, connecting to the right-side D of the previous triangle, and adding 1 bicone between Triangles 3 and 4; do not trim the thread.

FIG. 1: Rounds 1 and 2 of Triangle 1

FIG. 2: Working herringbone stitches and adding cubes

FIG. 3: Adding the nets

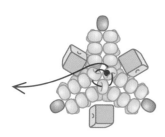

FIG. 4: Joining the nets to form the three-dimensional triangle

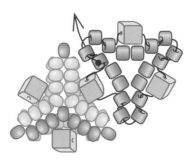

FIG. 5: Stitching Triangle 2 to Triangle 1's side D

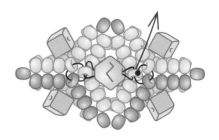

FIG. 6: Adding a crystal between Triangles 1 and 2

PEARL: Weave through beads to exit the 1A of Round 4 at the top of Triangle 4, away from the beadwork. String 1B, 1 pearl, and 1B; pass through the 1A at the top of Triangle 1. String 1B; pass through the 1A at the top of Triangle 2. String 1B; pass through the 1A at the top of Triangle 3. String 1B; pass through the 1A at the top of Triangle 4. Repeat the thread path to reinforce and weave through beads to exit 1A at the rightmost corner of Triangle 4 (FIG. 7).

3 Link

Use the working thread to peyote-stitch a link from the basket to the connector:

ROWS 1 AND 2: String 15B and pass through 1D of the connector triangle. String 15B and pass through the 1A at the leftmost corner of Triangle 1 (FIG. 8).

ROW 3: Pass back through the last B added and work 7 stitches with 1A in each stitch along the last set of 15B added in the previous row. Pass through the nearest 1B, the 1D, and the next 1B. Work 7 stitches with 1A in each stitch along the first set of 15B from the previous row (FIG. 9).

CRYSTAL: Weave through the first set of 15B to exit the fourteenth B (a down bead before the D). String 1B, 1 bicone, and 1B. Pass through the second B in the second set of 15B and pass back through the 1B/bicone/1B and the fourteenth B (FIG. 10). Weave through all the beads added in this step to reinforce. Secure the thread and trim.

4 Assembly

Slide an ear wire through the top corner of the connector.

5 Repeat Steps 1–4 for a second earring.

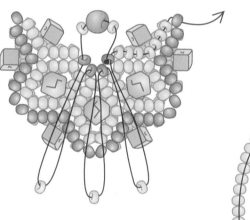

FIG. 7: Adding the pearl to the top of the basket

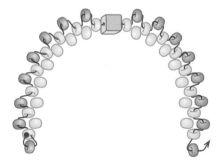

FIG. 9: Peyote-stitching along the link

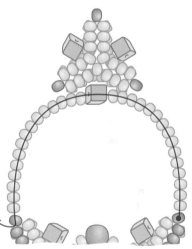

FIG. 8: Linking the basket and the connector

FIG. 10: Adding the crystal embellishment

Artist's Tips

- To create a hexagonal component that can be used for many other design options, work two more triangles to connect Triangles 1 and 4. One option would be to connect the hexagonal medallions into a bracelet.

- Don't be tempted to tie a knot after working Round 1; your subsequent thread passes will be difficult, and you may risk breaking your base cylinder beads in successive beading.

- Use triangle beads instead of cubes for a slightly different look.

12

Heliotrope

Reem Iversen

techniques

Tubular right-angle weave

Tubular peyote stitch

Circular herringbone stitch

materials

3 g metallic dark bronze size 15° seed beads (A)

2 g metallic dark bronze size 11° seed beads (B)

2 g hematite 5×2.5mm 2-hole seed beads (C)

2 hematite 8mm rounds (D)

1 pair of antiqued copper 12×16mm lever-back ear wires

Smoke 6 lb braided beading thread

Thread conditioner

tools

Scissors

Size 11 beading needle

FINISHED SIZE: 1⅞" (4.8cm)

① Bezel

Use right-angle weave and peyote stitch to bezel an 8mm round:

ROUND 1, UNIT 1: Use 6' (1.8m) of conditioned thread to string 4B, leaving a 3' (91.5cm) tail; pass through the first 3B (FIG. 1, BLUE THREAD).

ROUND 1, UNIT 2: String 3B; pass through the last B exited in the previous unit and the first 2B just added (FIG. 1, RED THREAD).

ROUND 1, UNITS 3–10: Repeat Unit 2 eight times.

ROUND 1, UNIT 11: String 1B; pass through the end B of Unit 1, making sure the beadwork isn't twisted. String 1B; pass through the last B exited in the previous unit, the first B just added, and the next 3B of Unit 1 (FIG. 2).

FOCAL BEAD: String 1D and place it into the bezel; pass down through a side B on the opposite side of the bezel. *NOTE: Since the bezel has an odd number of units, there is not an exact opposite B so choose the nearest bead.* Pass back through the D and up through the last B exited in Unit 1. Repeat the thread path to reinforce. Pass through the top B of the next unit (FIG. 3). At this point the tail and working threads are exiting opposite sides of Round 1. *NOTE: The D will fit loosely into the bezel at this point.*

ROUND 2: String 1B and pass through the next top B of Round 1; repeat ten times to work tubular peyote stitch around the top edge of the bezel. Step up by passing up through the first bead added in the current round (FIG. 4). Remove the needle from the working thread.

ROUND 3: Turn the beadwork over and add the needle to the tail thread. Pass through the next bottom B of Round 1. Repeat Round 2 on the back of the bezel, working off of the bottom B of Round 1. Remove the needle from the tail thread.

② Front

Use circular herringbone stitch to form the front of the earring:

ROUND 4: Add the needle to the working thread (the thread exiting Round 2 on the front of the bezel). String 2A and pass through the next B; repeat ten times. Step up by passing up through the first bead added in this round (FIG. 5, BLUE THREAD).

ROUND 5: String 2A, pass down through the next A of the previous round, the nearest B, and up through the following A; repeat ten times. Step up by passing through the first bead added in this round (FIG. 5, RED THREAD).

ROUND 6: String 2A and pass down through the next A of the previous round, then string 1B and pass up through the following A of the previous round; repeat ten times. Step up by passing through the first A added in this round (FIG. 6, ORANGE THREAD).

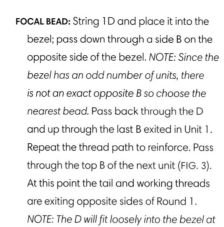

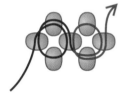

FIG. 1: Forming Units 1 and 2 of Round 1

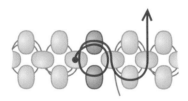

FIG. 2: Connecting the ends of Round 1

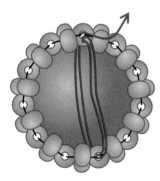

FIG. 3: Attaching the 8mm round bead to the bezel

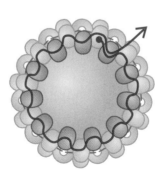

FIG. 4: Peyote-stitching Round 2

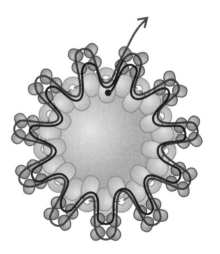

FIG. 5: Stitching Rounds 4 and 5

ROUND 7: String 2A and pass down through the next A of the previous round, through the nearest B of the previous round, and up through the following A of the previous round; repeat ten times. Step up by passing through the first A added in this round (FIG. 6, PURPLE THREAD).

ROUND 8: String 2A and pass down through the next A of the previous round, then string 1C and pass up through the following A of the previous round; repeat ten times. Step up by passing through the first bead added in this round (FIG. 6, GREEN THREAD). *NOTE: The beadwork will begin to cup; keep thread tension tight to allow the beadwork to continue to cup until the end of Round 10.*

ROUND 9: String 2A and pass down through the next A of the previous round, the same (inside) hole of the nearest C, and up through the following A of the previous round; repeat ten times. Step up by passing through the first A added in this round (FIG. 6, BLUE THREAD).

ROUND 10: String 1A; pass down through the next A of the previous round. String 1A; pass through the second (outside) hole of the nearest C. String 1A; pass up through the next A of the previous round. Repeat from the beginning of this round ten times. Pass through the first A added in this round (FIG. 6, RED THREAD). Remove the needle from the working thread.

③ Back

Use circular herringbone stitch to form the back of the earring:

ROUNDS 11–14: Turn the beadwork over and add the needle to the tail thread. Repeat Rounds 4–7. Pass down through the next A.

ROUND 15: String 2A and pass down through the next A of the previous round, pass through the inside hole of the nearest C of Round 8, and pass up through the next A of the previous round; repeat ten times. *NOTE: This connects the back layer to the front.* Gently press on the 2 layers as you stitch through the C beads to roll out the cupped edges of the front layer of the beadwork. Your finished component should have a slightly raised dome-shaped front; the back layer will lay flat. Secure the tail thread and trim.

④ Ear Wire

Add the needle to the working thread. String 8A, an ear wire, and 3A; pass back through the fifth A added. String 4A; pass through the next A of Round 10 (FIG. 7). Weave through beads to repeat the thread path several times to reinforce. Secure the thread and trim.

⑤ Repeat Steps 1–4 for a second earring.

Artist's Tips

- For a more defined bezel, choose a different color for the size 11° seed beads.

- 5x3mm Twin two-hole seed beads will work in place of the 5x2.5mm SuperDuo two-hole seed beads.

- Substitute a matte round glass pearl for the 8mm round to create a vintage-style earring.

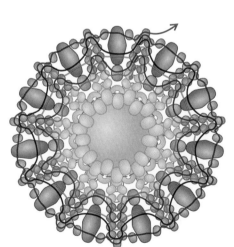

FIG. 6: Workings Rounds 6–10

FIG. 7: Attaching an ear wire

Blue Jean Queen

Barbara Falkowitz

technique

Circular peyote stitch

materials

1 g matte green/gray size 11° seed beads (A)

16 opaque blue/green Picasso 5×2.5mm 2-hole seed beads (B)

4 bronze 3×2mm crystal rondelles (C)

4 aqua AB 4×3mm crystal rondelles (D)

2 metallic bronze 12mm 2-hole bead studs (E)

2 antiqued brass 6mm twisted jump rings

1 pair of antiqued brass 14×16mm French ear wires

Smoke 6 lb braided beading thread

tools

Scissors

Size 10 beading needle

2 pairs of chain- or flat-nose pliers

FINISHED SIZE: 2" (5cm)

① Earrings

Use circular peyote stitch to form the earring base and fan-shaped embellishment:

BASE AND ROUND 1: Add a stop bead to 3' (91.5cm) of thread, leaving a 6" (15cm) tail. String 1E (left hole), 1A, 4B, and 1A; pass through the right hole of the E (FIG. 1, BLUE THREAD). String 2A, 1D, 2A, 1 jump ring, and 2A; pass back through the D just added. String 2A; pass through the E (left hole) and the next A (FIG. 1, RED THREAD). Weave through all the beads again to reinforce, exiting from the same A just exited. *NOTE: The beads below the E form Round 1.*

ROUND 2: String 2A; pass through the second (bottom) hole of the first B added in Round 1. String 1B; pass through the bottom hole of the following B. String 2B; pass through the bottom hole of the next B. String 1B; pass through the bottom hole of the last B. String 2A; pass through the second A added in Round 1. Pass through the E (right hole) and weave through beads to exit the first 2A added in this round (FIG. 2, BLUE THREAD).

ROUND 3: String 3A; pass through the bottom hole of the first B added in Round 2. String 1C; pass through the following B (bottom hole). String 1D; pass through the next B (bottom hole). String 1C; pass through the last B added in Round 2 (bottom hole). String 3A; pass through the nearest 3A on the outside edge of the fan and the E (right hole) (FIG. 2, RED THREAD). Remove the stop bead; secure the threads and trim.

② Ear Wire

Use a jump ring to attach an ear wire to the top loop.

③ Repeat Steps 1 and 2 for a second earring.

Artist's Tips

- Use a contrasting color for the stop bead so you don't accidentally incorporate it into the beadwork.

- For the earring to hang correctly, it's important to center the beads of the top loop above the bead stud and to maintain tight tension.

FIG. 1: Creating the base and Round 1

FIG. 2: Stitching Rounds 2 and 3

Floret

Tina Häuer

technique
Circular peyote stitch

materials

44 metallic gold size 15° seed beads (A)

12 metallic gold size 8° seed beads (B)

12 rainbow-frosted transparent olivine size 8° seed beads (C)

12 matte gold 5×2.5mm 2-hole seed beads (D)

24 opaque olive 5×2.5mm 2-hole seed beads (E)

1 pair of gold-plated 17mm ear wires

Smoke 10 lb braided beading thread

tools

Scissors or thread burner

Size 12 or 13 beading needle

FINISHED SIZE: 2" (5cm)

① Body

Use circular peyote stitch to form the body of the earring:

ROUND 1: Use 4' (1.2m) of thread to string 6C, leaving a 4" (10cm) tail. Use the working and tail threads to tie a knot, forming a tight circle. Pass through the first C strung (FIG. 1, GREEN THREAD).

ROUND 2: String 1D, then pass through the next C of Round 1; repeat five times. Pass through the first (inside) hole, then the second (outside) hole of the first D in this round (FIG. 1, BLUE THREAD). *NOTE: You will now begin stitching in the opposite direction.*

ROUND 3: String 1E, 1B, and 1E, then pass through the outside hole of the next D in Round 2; repeat five times. Pass through all the beads of this round again, then pass through the outside hole of the last E exited (FIG. 1, RED THREAD).

② Ear Wire

String 18A and an ear wire; skip the last 5A strung and pass back through the next 9A (FIG. 2, BLUE THREAD). String 4A; pass through the outside hole of the last E exited (FIG. 2, RED THREAD). Repeat the thread path to reinforce; secure the threads and trim.

③ Repeat Steps 1 and 2 for a second earring.

variation

If you dislike the exposed outside holes of the SuperDuos, work Round 3 using Super-Unos instead. Connect the ear wire to the hole of a SuperUno as in Step 2, increasing the number of beads used as needed.

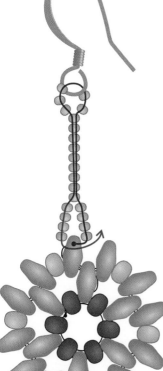

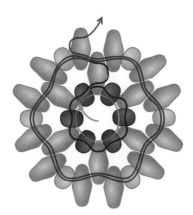

FIG. 1: Forming the earring body

FIG. 2: Adding the ear wire

Artist's Tip

- Use a thread burner instead of scissors to cut the thread as close to the beadwork as possible.

MAIN COLORWAY

Floral Swirl

Cheryl Erickson

techniques

Circular square stitch

Netting

Wireworking

materials

2 g matte light olive size 11° seed beads (A)

2 g matte fuchsia size 11° seed beads (B)

2 g matte light olive rainbow size 11° seed beads (C)

2 g matte dark forest green size 11° seed beads (D)

1 g matte light olive rainbow size 8° seed beads (E)

2 matte cream 13mm pressed-glass rings

1 pair of copper ¾" (2cm) ear wires

Crystal 6 lb braided beading thread

tools

Scissors

Size 10 or 11 beading needle

2 pairs of chain-nose pliers

FINISHED SIZE: 2" (5cm)

❶ Medallion

Use circular square stitch and netted fringe to form the earring's medallion:

ROUND 1: Tie the end of 4' (122cm) of thread to 1 ring, leaving a 6" (15cm) tail. String 2E; pass through the ring back to front and through the second E just added, leaving the 2E on the outside of the ring (FIG. 1, GREEN THREAD). String 1E; pass through the ring back to front and through the E just added. Continue working circular square stitch, 1E at a time, around the ring for a total of 22E or for an even number of E that fit snugly around the ring (FIG. 1, BLUE THREAD). Pass through all the E added in this round again to reinforce, exiting from the first E added (FIG. 1, RED THREAD).

ROUND 2: String 7A, skip 1E of Round 1, and pass through the next E; repeat ten times. Pass through the next E of Round 1, toward the back of the work (FIG. 2).

ROUND 3: String 5B, pass over the beads of the next loop, skip 1E of Round 1, and pass through the following E toward the back of the work; repeat ten times. Manipulate the new nets so they sit snugly between the nets of Round 2. Step up for the next round by passing through the first 3B added in this round (FIG. 3).

ROUND 4: String 7C and pass through the middle B of the next Round 3 net; repeat ten times. Weave through beads to exit from the middle A of a Round 2 net so that the thread sits in front of a Round 4 net (FIG. 4, BLUE THREAD).

ROUND 5: String 5D, pass behind and through the next Round 4 net, and pass through the middle A and in front of the following Round 2 net (FIG. 4, RED THREAD); repeat ten times. Secure the thread and trim.

❷ Ear Wire

Use chain-nose pliers to connect an ear wire to 2 nets for extra strength.

❸ Repeat Steps 1 and 2 for a second earring.

FIG. 1: Stitching Round 1

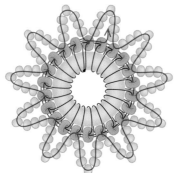

FIG. 2: Adding Round 2

Artist's Tips

- Be sure to use contrasting but coordinating colors to make the crisscross pattern show.

- Attach medallions in a row for a bracelet or a necklace.

- To make a large medallion for a pendant, continue adding crisscrossing nets and increasing bead counts each round.

FIG. 3: Forming Round 3

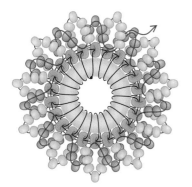

FIG. 4: Completing Round 4 and beginning Round 5

Halo

Lisa Kan

techniques

Tubular and circular peyote stitch

Picot

materials

2 g matte antiqued silver size 15º Japanese seed beads (A)

2 g medium amethyst rainbow size 15º Japanese seed beads (B)

3 g semiglazed blue turquoise size 11º Japanese seed beads (C)

1 g matte antiqued silver size 11º Japanese seed beads (D)

1 pair of sterling silver 11×18mm ear wires with 3mm ball

Smoke 6 lb FireLine braided beading thread

tools

Scissors

Size 12 beading needle

No-tangle bobbin (optional)

FINISHED SIZE: 2" (5cm)

Ring

Use tubular peyote stitch to create the earring base ring:

RING ROUNDS 1 AND 2: Use 8' (2.4m) of thread to string 52C, leaving a 2' (61cm) tail. Use the working and tail threads to tie a square knot, forming a circle. *NOTE: Step up for this and subsequent rounds by passing through the first bead added in the current round unless otherwise indicated* (FIG. 1, BLUE THREAD). Make sure the square knot doesn't slip inside the first C. *NOTE: You may use a no-tangle bobbin to keep the tail thread out of your way for the following rounds.*

RING ROUNDS 3–5: Work 26 stitches with 1C in each stitch; repeat twice (FIG. 1, RED THREAD).

RING ROUNDS 6–12: Work 26 stitches with 1A in each stitch; repeat six times (FIG. 2).

ZIP: Fold the beadwork so that Ring Rounds 1 and 12 interlock like a zipper. Pass through the nearest C of Ring Round 1 and the following A of Ring Round 12 (FIG. 3, BLUE THREAD; beadwork flattened for clarity); repeat twenty-five times to form a seamless tube. Exit from the nearest C of Ring Round 1 (FIG. 3, RED THREAD).

 Embellishments

Use circular peyote stitch and picots to embellish the base ring:

SURFACE LOOPS: *NOTE: Make sure you're exiting to the right from 1C of Ring Round 1.* *Working counterclockwise around the ring, string 9B, skip the next C of Ring Round 1, and pass through the following C of Ring Round 1 with your needle passing through the C from left to right (FIG. 4, GREEN THREAD). String 1B; pass through the C of Ring Round 1 just skipped from left to right (FIG. 4, BLUE THREAD). Repeat from * twenty-five times for a total of 26 loops, making sure each new loop rests on top of the previous loop (FIG. 4, RED THREAD). *NOTE: On the twenty-fourth loop, pass the needle under Loop 1 before passing through the C in Ring Round 1; repeat on the twenty-fifth loop, passing the needle under Loops 1 and 2 before passing through the C in Ring Round 1. Weave through beads to exit from the nearest C of Ring Round 3.*

EDGE ROUND 1: Turn the beadwork over. String 1D and pass through the next C of Ring Round 3; repeat twenty-five times. Step up through the first D added in this round (FIG. 5, BLUE THREAD; back of beadwork shown). *NOTE: The D added in this round are stitched in the ditch between Ring Rounds 2 and 4.*

EDGE ROUND 2: String 1C and pass through the next D of Edge Round 1; repeat twenty-five times. Step up through the first C added in this round and the nearest D of Edge Round 1 (FIG. 5, RED THREAD).

EDGE ROUND 3: String 3A and pass through the last D exited, the next C of Edge Round 2, and the following D of Edge Round 1 to form a picot; repeat twenty-five times, but don't pass through the final D after the last repeat. Pass back through the 3A of the first picot added (FIG. 6, GREEN THREAD; back of beadwork shown). Pass back through the 3A of the nearest picot; repeat twenty-five times. Pass back through the nearest 2A of the following picot (FIG. 6, BLUE THREAD).

EAR-WIRE LOOP: String 5A; pass back through the second and first A of the next picot in Edge Round 3 (FIG. 6, RED THREAD). Tie a half-hitch knot, form a turnaround, and pass back through the last 9A exited to reinforce the loop; repeat. Secure the working thread and trim.

❸ Finishing

Turn the beadwork over. Add a needle to the tail thread and weave counterclockwise through beads to exit from the nearest C of Edge Round 2. *NOTE: The starting direction of the thread path in this step should match the direction of the surface loops.* Pass through the end B of the nearest surface loop and through the next C of Edge Round 2; repeat twenty-five times (FIG. 7). Secure the thread and trim. Attach an ear wire to the ear-wire loop.

❹ Repeat Steps 1–3 for a second earring.

Artist's Tips

- Depending on the seed bead manufacturer and your beading tension, the size of your earring may vary slightly.

- Create graduated earring components and connect them to make a bracelet or necklace. Always start the ring with an even number of beads.

FIG. 1: Working Ring Rounds 1–5

FIG. 2: Adding Ring Rounds 6–12

FIG. 3: Zipping the ring

FIG. 4: Adding the surface loops

FIG. 5: Forming Edge Rounds 1 and 2

FIG. 6: Stitching Edge Round 3 and the ear-wire loop

FIG. 7: Finishing the earring

Fire & Ice

Monica Corsaro

techniques

Circular peyote stitch

Netting

materials

5 g starlight galvanized permanent-finish size 15°
Japanese seed beads (A)

3 g starlight galvanized permanent-finish size 11°
Japanese seed beads (B)

24 air blue opal 3mm crystal bicones (C)

28 crystal astral pink 4mm crystal bicones (D)

28 aquamarine opal AB 4mm fire-polished rounds (E)

2 crystal astral pink 5×10mm crystal navettes in gold-color
metal settings (F)

1 pair of gold-filled 14k 22×17mm ear wires

White size B nylon beading thread

tools

Scissors

Size 11 or 12 beading needles

FINISHED SIZE: 2⅛" (5.4cm)

1 Circle

ROUND 1: Use 6' (1.8m) of thread to string {3A and 1B} fourteen times, leaving an 18" (45.5cm) tail; pass through the beads again to form a circle. Use the working and tail threads to tie a knot. Pass through the first 3A/1B strung (FIG. 1, GREEN THREAD).

ROUND 2: String 1A, 1E, and 1B; pass back through the E just added. String 1A; pass through the next B of Round 1. Repeat from the beginning of this round thirteen times. Step up through the first B added in this round (FIG. 1, BLUE THREAD).

ROUND 3: String 1A, 1D, and 1A; pass through the next B of Round 2. String 1B, 1D, and 1B; pass through the following B of Round 2. Repeat from the beginning of this round six times (FIG. 1, RED THREAD).

ROUND 4: String 4A; pass through the nearest B of Round 1. String 4A; pass through the following B of Round 2 (FIG. 2, BLUE THREAD). Repeat from the beginning of this round thirteen times to frame each E of Round 2 (FIG. 2, RED THREAD).

ROUND 5: Turn the beadwork over so the front is facedown. Repeat Round 4, this time framing the back side of each E of Round 2. Weave through beads to exit from the B of Round 1 next to the tail thread. Set the working thread aside.

2 Center

STITCH 1: Turn the beadwork over so the front is faceup. Add a needle to the tail thread. String 7A, 1F (faceup), and 7A; skip 3A/1B/3A of Round 1 and pass through the next B of Round 1. Weave through beads to exit from the fifth B from the last B exited (FIG. 3, BLUE THREAD).

STITCH 2: String 7A; pass through the second (bottom) hole of the F in Stitch 1. String 7A; skip 3A/1B/3A of Round 1 and pass through the following B of Round 1. Weave through beads to exit from the first set of 7A (upper-left strand) added in Stitch 1 (FIG. 3, RED THREAD).

STITCH 3: String 1C; pass down through the top 4A of the lower-left strand of Stitch 2 (FIG. 4, ORANGE THREAD).

STITCH 4: String 1A, 1C, and 1A; pass back through the nearest B of Round 1 (between the bottom 2 strands of 7A) (FIG. 4, GREEN THREAD).

STITCH 5: String 1A, 1C, and 1A; pass up through the top 4A of the lower-right strand of Stitch 2 (FIG. 4, BLUE THREAD).

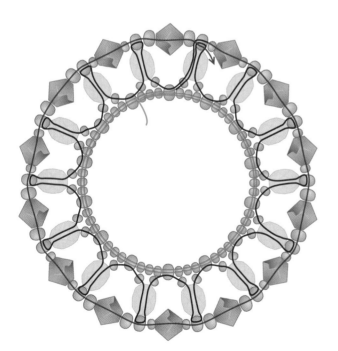

FIG. 1: Forming Rounds 1–3 of the circle

FIG. 2: Adding Round 4 of the circle

STITCH 6: String 1C; pass up through the bottom 4A of the upper-right strand of Stitch 1.

STITCH 7: String 1A, 1C, and 1A; pass back through the nearest B of Round 1 (between the top 2 strands of 7A).

STITCH 8: String 1A, 1C, and 1A; pass down through the bottom 4A of the upper-left strand of Stitch 1 (FIG. 4, RED THREAD).

STITCH 9: String 4A; pass down through the top 4A of the lower-left strand of Stitch 2, then weave through beads to exit up through the top 4A of the lower-right strand of Stitch 2 (FIG. 5, BLUE THREAD).

STITCH 10: String 4A; pass up through the bottom 4A of the upper-right strand of Stitch 1, then weave through beads to exit down through the second 1A/1C/1A set added in Stitch 8 (upper-left set) (FIG. 5, RED THREAD).

STITCH 11: String 1C and 2A; pass down through the 4A of Stitch 9 (FIG. 6, ORANGE THREAD). String 2A and 1C; pass down through the lower-left 1A/1C/1A set of Stitch 4 and weave through beads to exit up through the lower-right 1A/1C/1A set of Stitch 5 (FIG. 6, GREEN THREAD). String 1C and 2A; pass up through the 4A of Stitch 10 (FIG. 6, BLUE THREAD). String 2A and 1C; pass up through the upper-right 1A/1C/1A set of Stitch 7. Weave through beads, forming a turnaround as necessary, to exit up through the bottom A of the upper-left 1A/1C/1A set of Stitch 8 (FIG. 6, RED THREAD).

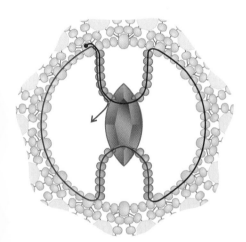

FIG. 3: Working Stitches 1 and 2 of the center

FIG. 4: Adding Stitches 3–8 of the center

FIG. 5: Forming Stitches 9 and 10 of the center

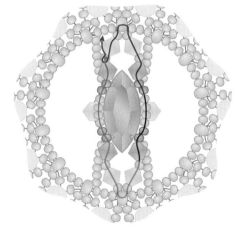

FIG. 6: Working Stitch 11 of the center

Artist's Tips

- Keeping even tension is key for a successful project.

- Be sure to cull your seed beads so that they are consistent in size.

- For a different look, replace the crystal bicones with pearl rounds.

STITCH 12: String 1A, 1C, and 1A; pass down through the 8A along the right side of the F (FIG. 7, PURPLE THREAD).

STITCH 13: String 1A, 1C, and 1A; pass down through the lower-left 1A/1C/1A set of Stitch 4, pass through the next B, and pass up through the lower-right 1A/1C/1A set of Stitch 5 (FIG. 7, ORANGE THREAD).

STITCH 14: String 1A; pass back through the C of Stitch 13. String 1A; pass up through the 8A along the left side of the F (FIG. 7, GREEN THREAD).

STITCH 15: String 1A and pass back up through the C of Stitch 12 (directly above the F) (FIG. 7, BLUE THREAD).

STITCH 16: String 1A; pass up through the upper-right 1A/1C/1A set of Stitch 7 and weave through beads to exit down through the 10A along the left side of the F (FIG. 7, RED THREAD).

STITCH 17: String 2A; pass up through the 10A along the right side of the F (FIG. 8, BLUE THREAD; other center beads not shown for clarity).

STITCH 18: String 2A; pass down through the 10A along the left side of the F (FIG. 8, RED THREAD). Weave through all 24A surrounding the F again to reinforce. Secure and trim this tail thread.

③ Loop

Add a needle to the original working thread and weave through beads to exit from the 1A/1D/1A set of Round 3 that sits directly above the center. String 5B and pass through the last 1A/1D/1A set exited to form a loop (FIG. 9); repeat the thread path to reinforce. Secure the thread and trim. Add an ear wire to the loop just formed by opening and closing the ear-wire loop as you would a jump ring, ensuring the navette faces forward when worn.

④ Repeat Steps 1–3 for a second earring.

FIG. 7: Adding Stitches 12–16 of the center

FIG. 8: Forming Stitches 17 and 18 of the center

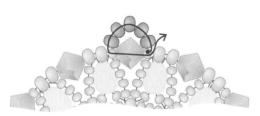

FIG. 9: Adding the loop

Coachella

Melinda Barta

techniques

Odd-count flat peyote stitch variation

materials

16 metallic bronze size 15° Japanese seed beads (A)

24 opaque pyrite Picasso 6×3mm 2-hole bricks (B)

8 metallic bronze 6×3mm 2-hole bricks (C)

1 pair of matte antiqued brass 16×17mm ear wires

9¾" (25cm) of brass 1×1.5mm oval chain

Smoke 6 lb braided beading thread

tools

Scissors

Size 10 beading needle

Wire cutter

FINISHED SIZE: 2¾" (7cm)

1 Body

Use odd-count flat peyote stitch to form the body of the earring:

ROWS 1 AND 2: Use 2' (61cm) of thread to string 2B, 3C, and 2B, leaving an 8" (20.5cm) tail. Step up by passing through the second hole of the last B added (FIG. 1, GREEN THREAD).

ROW 3: String 1B; skip 1B of the previous row and pass through the second (top) hole of the following C. String 1C; skip 1C of the previous row and pass through the second (top) hole of the following C. String 1B; skip 1B of the previous row and pass through the second (top) hole of the following B. Use the working and tail threads to tie a knot (FIG. 1, BLUE THREAD). Weave back through the top holes of Row 2 and the bottom holes of Row 3 to exit from the top hole of the first B added in this row, toward the work (FIG. 1, RED THREAD).

ROW 4: String 1B; pass through the top hole of the C in Row 3. String 1B; pass through the top hole of the next B in Row 3 (FIG. 2, PURPLE THREAD). Weave back through the bottom holes of Row 3 and the top holes of Row 2 to exit from the bottom hole of the first B in Row 3, away from the work (FIG. 2, GREEN THREAD). Weave through the top holes of Row 3 and the bottom holes of Row 4 to exit from the top hole of the second B added in this row, toward the work (FIG. 2, BLUE THREAD).

ROW 5: String 1B; pass through the top hole of the next B in Row 4 (FIG. 2, RED THREAD).

ROWS 6 AND 7: Rotate the work 180 degrees and weave through beads to exit from the top hole of the first B in Row 1, toward the beadwork (FIG. 3, BLUE THREAD). *NOTE: Because the work has been rotated, the holes that were top holes are now bottom holes, and vice versa.* Repeat Rows 4 and 5 (FIG. 3, RED THREAD).

2 Ear Wire

Weave through beads to exit the top hole of the B in Row 7 (FIG. 4, BLUE THREAD). String 4A, an ear wire, and 4A, then pass through the top hole of the last B exited (FIG. 4, RED THREAD); repeat the thread path several times to reinforce. Secure the working thread and trim.

3 Chains

Add swags of chain to the bottom half of the earring body:

LONG CHAIN: Add a needle to the tail thread. String one end of one 3" (7.5cm) piece of chain; pass back through the bottom hole of the last B exited. Weave through beads to exit from the bottom hole of the last B in Row 2. String the other end of the chain; pass back through the bottom hole of the last B exited (FIG. 5, GREEN THREAD). Weave through beads to exit from the bottom hole of the second B in Row 4, away from the work (FIG. 5, BLUE THREAD).

FIG. 1: Forming Rows 1–3 of the earring body

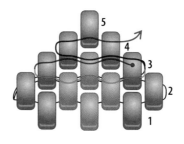

FIG. 2: Adding Rows 4 and 5

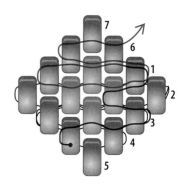

FIG. 3: Working Rows 6 and 7

SHORT CHAIN: String one end of one 1¾" (4.5cm) piece of chain; pass back through the bottom hole of the last B exited. Weave through beads to exit from the bottom hole of the first B in Row 4, away from the work. String the other end of the chain; pass back through the bottom hole of the last B exited (FIG. 5, RED THREAD). Weave through beads to repeat both chain connections. Secure the tail thread and trim.

④ Repeat Steps 1–3 for a second earring.

Artist's Tips

- Use relaxed tension when weaving through beads to help preserve the openness between bricks.

- Though you could form the body of the earring by working odd-count peyote-stitch thread-loop turnarounds at the end of each row, using the method shown here maintains nice, even spaces between the bricks.

FIG. 4: Attaching the ear wire

FIG. 5: Adding the chains

Dancing Birch

Agnieszka Watts

techniques

Netting

Picot

Fringe

materials

3 g dark purple size 15° seed beads (A)

1 g galvanized gold size 15° seed beads (B)

14 gold aurum 3mm crystal bicones (C)

4 gold aurum 4mm crystal bicones (D)

4 light Colorado topaz AB 4mm crystal rounds (E)

4 vintage gold 3mm crystal pearl rounds (F)

18 vintage gold 4mm crystal pearl rounds (G)

2 antiqued brass 6mm crystal pearl rounds (H)

2 antiqued brass 8mm crystal pearl rounds (I)

2 antiqued brass 7×11mm crystal pearl drops (J)

1 pair of gold-plated ¾" (2cm) ear wires

Black size D nylon beading thread

tools

Scissors

Size 12 or 13 beading needle

Thread burner

FINISHED SIZE: 3¾" (9.5cm)

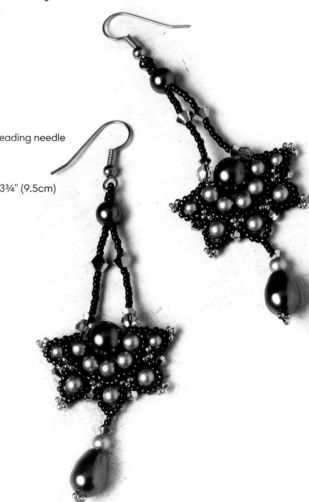

① Body

Use netting, picot, and fringe techniques to form the earring's body:

BASE: Use 3' (91.5cm) of thread to string 1I and 3G, leaving a 3" (7.5cm) tail; pass through the beads again and exit through the I (FIG. 1, BLUE THREAD). String 1G; pass back through the I. String 1G; pass through the I and back through the nearest G (FIG. 1, RED THREAD).

ROW 1: String 6A and pass through the last G exited and the next G (FIG. 2, GREEN THREAD); repeat four times to encircle all the G with A (FIG. 2, BLUE THREAD). Pass through all the A just strung again to reinforce, then pass through the 5G and the nearest 5A (FIG. 2, RED THREAD).

ROW 2: String 3B, skip 2A of Row 1, and pass through the next 4A; repeat twice. String 3B, skip 2A of Row 1, and pass through the next 3A (FIG. 3).

ROW 3: String 2A, 1F, and 2A; pass through the center B of the nearest 3B net in Row 2. String 2A, 1G, and 2A, then pass back through the center B of the next 3B net in Row 2; repeat twice. String 2A, 1F, and 2A; pass back through the first 2A of the nearest 6A net in Row 1 (FIG. 4).

HANGING LOOP: String 1E, 1C, 9A, 1D, 6A, 1H, 4A, an ear wire, and 4A; pass back through the H. String 6A, 1D, 9A, 1C, and 1E; pass down through the top 2A of Row 1 on the other side of the body. Weave through beads to exit from the nearest F of Row 3, toward the center of the beadwork (FIG. 5).

FIG. 1: Forming the earring base

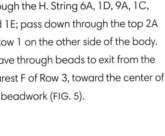

FIG. 2: Stitching Row 1

FIG. 3: Adding Row 2

FIG. 4: Forming Row 3

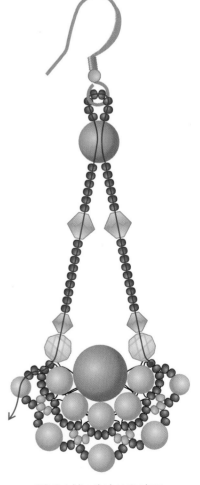

FIG. 5: Adding the hanging loop

ROW 4, STITCH 1: String 5A; pass through the last F exited and the nearest A of Row 3 (FIG. 6, BLACK THREAD).

ROW 4, STITCH 2: String 1C, skip 2A of Row 3, and pass through the next 1A/1G. String 7A; pass through the last 1A/1G exited and the nearest 1A of Row 3 (FIG. 6, ORANGE THREAD).

ROW 4, STITCHES 3 AND 4: Repeat Row 4, Stitch 2, twice (FIG. 6, GREEN THREAD).

ROW 4, STITCH 5: String 1C, skip 2A of Row 3, and pass through the next 1A/1G. String 5A; pass through the last 1A/1G exited and the first 3A just added (FIG. 6, BLUE THREAD).

ROW 5: String 3B, pass through the last A exited to form a picot, and weave through Row 4 beads to exit from the center A of the next 7A net; repeat to add a picot to Row 4, Stitch 4, and to exit the center of Row 4, Stitch 3. String 2A, 1C, 1G, 1J, and 3B; pass back through the 1J/1G/1C/2A, through the next 3A of Row 4, Stitch 3, and the fourth A of the 7A net in Row 4, Stitch 2, to form the center dangle. Weave through Row 4 beads to exit from the center A of the next 7A net. In the same manner, add 3B picots to Row 4, Stitches 2 and 1 (FIG. 6, RED THREAD). Weave through all the beads of Rows 4 and 5 again to reinforce. Secure the thread and trim.

2 Repeat Step 1 for a second earring.

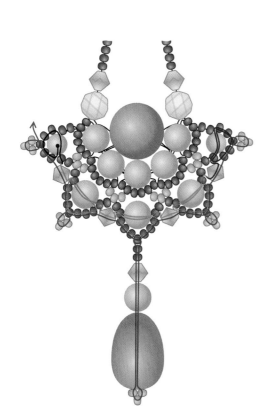

FIG. 6: Stitching Rows 4 and 5 and the center dangle

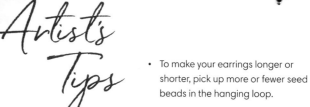

- To make your earrings longer or shorter, pick up more or fewer seed beads in the hanging loop.

- Agnieszka used Nymo black size D in this project but recommends the Nymo that comes on big spools rather than on bobbins. Although the threads are sold as the same type and size, she finds that the spooled type works better for beadwork because it's slightly heavier than the thread sold on bobbins.

Candlelight

Evelina Palmontová

techniques

Tubular peyote stitch

Netting

materials

1 g silver size 15° seed beads (A)

1 g gold size 11° cylinder beads (B)

36 jet AB2X 3mm crystal bicones (C)

30 crystal aurum 4mm bicones (D)

2 white 12mm pearl rounds

2 silver 17×20mm ear wires

White size B Nymo nylon beading thread

tools

Scissors

Size 11 beading needle

FINISHED SIZE: 2" (5cm)

1 Earring Back

Work tubular peyote stitch to form a bezel around the back of the pearl:

ROUNDS 1 AND 2: Use 6' (1.8m) of thread to string 1 pearl and 15B, leaving a 6" (15cm) tail; pass through the pearl and pull snug (FIG. 1, BLUE THREAD). String 15B; pass through the pearl and all of the B to form a circle of 30B around the pearl. Weave through beads to reach the tail thread; tie a knot with the working and tail threads and pass through the next B (FIG. 1, RED THREAD).

ROUND 3: String 1B, skip 1B of the previous round, and pass through the next B; repeat fourteen times. Step up for the next round by passing through the first B added in this round (FIG. 2, BLUE THREAD; shown flat for clarity).

ROUNDS 4 AND 5: Work 15 stitches with 1B in each stitch for 2 rounds. Step up through the first B of Round 5 (FIG. 2, RED THREAD).

ROUND 6: Work 15 stitches with 1A in each stitch. Pass through this round again, pulling the thread tight to snug the beads close to the pearl. Weave through beads to exit from Round 1 (FIG. 3, GREEN THREAD).

ROUND 7: Work 15 stitches with 1C in each stitch. Step up through the first C added in this round (FIG. 3, BLUE THREAD).

ROUND 8: Work 15 stitches with 1A in each stitch. Weave through beads to exit from Round 3 (FIG. 3, RED THREAD).

ROUND 9: String 1A and pass through the next B of Round 3; repeat fourteen times, adding 1A in the ditch above each C. Step up through the first A added in this round (FIG. 4, BLUE THREAD).

ROUND 10: String 1A, pass through the next A of Round 8 (between C beads), then string 1A and pass through the following A of Round 9; repeat fourteen times, forming little Vs around each C. Weave through beads to exit from 1A of Round 8, between the nearest 2C (FIG. 4, RED THREAD).

2 Earring Front

Embellish the front of the earring:

ROUND 11: Turn the beadwork over. String 3A, then pass through the last bead exited to form a net and pass through the next C of Round 7 and A of Round 8; repeat fourteen times. Step up through the first 2A added in this round (FIG. 5, BLUE THREAD). *NOTE: You'll now begin working in the opposite direction.*

ROUND 12: String 1D and pass through the middle A of the next 3A net; repeat fourteen times. Step up through the first D added in this round (FIG. 5, RED THREAD).

FIG. 1: Forming Rounds 1 and 2

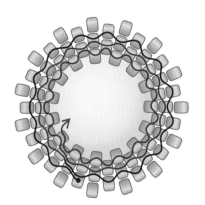

FIG. 2: Adding Rounds 3–5 (back view of earring)

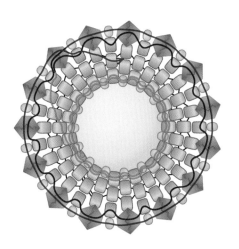

FIG. 3: Working Rounds 6–8 (back view of earring)

Ear Wire

String 1A, 3C, and 1A; pass through the last D exited, 1A, and the first 2C just added (FIG. 6, BLUE THREAD). String 4A, an ear wire (so that Rounds 4–6 are at the back of the earring), and 4A; pass through the last C exited and weave through beads to exit from the original D to form a tight loop (FIG. 6, RED THREAD). Repeat the thread path several times to reinforce. Secure the threads and trim.

4 Repeat Steps 1–3 for a second earring.

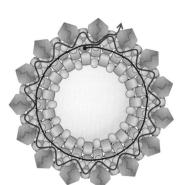

Artist's Tips

- You may replace the 12mm freshwater pearls with 12mm crystal or gemstone rounds.

- Both sides of the earrings are beautiful; wear them facing either way.

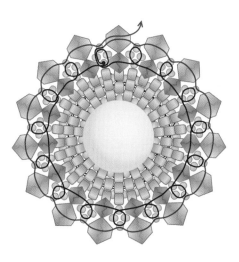

FIG. 4: Adding Rounds 9 and 10 (back view of earring)

FIG. 5: Stitching Rounds 11 and 12 (front view of earring)

FIG. 6: Adding the ear wire

21

Crystal Falls

Melissa Grakowsky Shippee

technique
Tubular peyote stitch

materials

1 g pewter galvanized size 15° Japanese seed beads (A)

1 g matte gold-lined aqua size 15° Japanese seed beads (B)

2 g nickel galvanized size 11° Japanese cylinder beads (C)

2 Pacific opal 4mm crystal bicones

2 foil-back Pacific opal 8×6mm pear-shaped crystal fancy stones

2 foil-back Pacific opal 14×10mm pear-shaped crystal fancy stones

2 silver-plated 4mm jump rings

1 pair of silver-plated 10×18mm lever-back ear wires

5" (12.5cm) of silver-plated 2×3mm oval chain

2½" (6.5cm) of gunmetal 2×3mm oval chain

Beige size D nylon beading thread

tools
Scissors

Size 12 beading needle

Wire cutters

2 pairs of chain- or flat-nose pliers

FINISHED SIZE: 3½" (9cm)

① Large Bezel

Use tubular peyote stitch to bezel a 14×10mm pear-shaped fancy stone:

ROUNDS 1 AND 2: Use 3' (91.5cm) of thread to string 31C, leaving a 4" (10cm) tail. Pass through the first 2C strung to form a circle (FIG. 1, GREEN THREAD).

ROUND 3: String 1C, skip 1C of the previous rounds, and pass through the next C; repeat fourteen times (FIG. 1, BLUE THREAD). String 1C; pass through the nearest C of Round 2 and the next C of Round 1 (FIG. 1, RED THREAD). *NOTE: The last C added will form the point of the bezel. Rounds 4 and 5 will form the front of the bezel, and Rounds 6–8 will form the back of the bezel.*

ROUND 4: Work 15 stitches with 1B in each stitch. Pass through the first B of this round (FIG. 2, GREEN THREAD).

ROUND 5: Work 15 stitches with 1A in each stitch (FIG. 2, BLUE THREAD). Weave through beads to exit from the third C of Round 3 (FIG. 2, RED THREAD). Flip the beadwork facedown. Place one 14×10mm pear-shaped fancy stone facedown into the beadwork so that the point of the stone touches the last C added in Round 3.

ROUND 6: Work 12 stitches with 1B in each stitch. String 2B; skip the next (point) C of Round 3 and pass through the next C. Work 2 stitches with 1B in each stitch. Pass through the first B of this round (FIG. 3, GREEN THREAD; back of beadwork is shown).

ROUND 7: Work 11 stitches with 1A in each stitch. String 1A; pass through the next 2B of the previous round at the point of the bezel. Work 3 stitches with 1A in each stitch. Step up through the first A of this round (FIG. 3, BLUE THREAD).

ROUND 8: Work 15 stitches with 1A in each stitch (FIG. 3, RED THREAD). Flip the work faceup. Weave through beads to exit up through the C of Round 2 marked with a blue start dot in FIG. 4. *NOTE: The beadwork is flipped faceup in Fig. 4.*

CONNECTION BEAD: String 1C; pass through the next C of Round 2 to stitch in the ditch (FIG. 4, BLUE THREAD). Weave through beads to form a turnaround and pass back through the C just added and the next C of Round 2 to reinforce (FIG. 4, RED THREAD); repeat twice. Weave through beads to exit from the C of Round 2 on the opposite edge of the bezel marked with a red start dot in FIG. 5.

EAR-WIRE LOOP: String 5A and pass through the last C exited (FIG. 5); repeat the thread path to reinforce. Secure the threads and trim. Set aside.

FIG. 1: Stitching Rounds 1–3 of the large bezel

FIG. 2: Working Rounds 4 and 5 of the large bezel

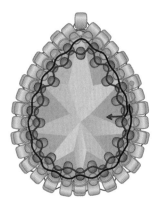

FIG. 3: Forming Rounds 6–8 of the large bezel

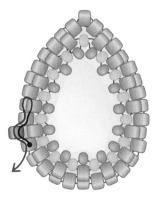

FIG. 4: Adding the connection bead to the large bezel

FIG. 5: Stitching the ear-wire loop on the large bezel

2 Medium Bezel

Use tubular peyote stitch to bezel an 8×6mm pear-shaped fancy stone:

ROUNDS 1 AND 2: Repeat Step 1, Rounds 1 and 2, this time stringing 19C.

ROUND 3: String 1C, skip 1C of the previous rounds, and pass through the next C; repeat eight times. String 1C; pass through the nearest C of Round 2 and the next C of Round 1. *NOTE: The last C added will form the point of the bezel. Round 4 will form the front of the bezel, and Rounds 5 and 6 will form the back of the bezel.*

ROUND 4: Work 9 stitches with 1A in each stitch. Weave through beads to exit from the second C of Round 3. Flip the beadwork facedown. Place one 8×6mm pear-shaped fancy stone facedown into the beadwork so that the point of the stone touches the last C added in Round 3.

ROUND 5: Work 7 stitches with 1A in each stitch. String 1A; skip the next (point) C of Round 3 and pass through the next C. Work 1 stitch with 1A. Pass through the first A of this round.

ROUND 6: Work 9 stitches with 1A in each stitch. Weave through beads to exit from 1C of Round 2, near the bottom curve of the pear. Flip the beadwork faceup.

CONNECTION BEAD: Repeat Step 1, Connection Bead. *NOTE: When the large bezel and the medium bezel are faceup, the connection bead should be added to the same (left) side of each bezel. Weave through beads to exit from the mirror C of Round 2 on the opposite edge of the bezel, near the bottom curve of the pear. Secure and trim the tail thread but don't trim the working thread. Set aside.*

FIG. 6: Forming Rounds 3 and 4 of the small bezel

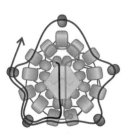

FIG. 7: Adding the center of the small bezel

Artist's Tip

- You can use any size chain for this project, but chain with small links is more proportionate to the seed beads used in the bezels.

3 Small Bezel

Use tubular peyote stitch to form a bezel around a bicone:

ROUNDS 1 AND 2: Repeat Step 1, Rounds 1 and 2, this time stringing 12C.

ROUND 3: Work 2 stitches with 1A in each stitch. String 2A; skip the next 2C of the previous rounds and pass through the next C. Work 2 stitches with 1A in each stitch (FIG. 6, GREEN THREAD). String 1C; pass through the next C of the previous rounds and the first A of this round (FIG. 6, BLUE THREAD). *NOTE: The last C added will form the point of the bezel. Rounds 3 and 4 will form the back of the bezel, and Round 5 will form the front of the bezel.*

ROUND 4: String 1A; pass through the next A of the previous round. String 1A; pass through the next 2A of the previous round. String 1A and pass through the next A of the previous round; repeat. String 2A; pass through the next A of the previous round and weave through beads to exit from the seventh C of Rounds 1 and 2, opposite the point (FIG. 6, RED THREAD). Flip the beadwork facedown.

CENTER: String 1 bicone; pass back through the opposite 2C of Rounds 1 and 2, skipping the nearest (point) C of Round 3 (FIG. 7, GREEN THREAD). Pass back through the bicone and the next C of Rounds 1 and 2 (FIG. 7, BLUE THREAD).

ROUND 5: Work 2 stitches with 1A in each stitch. String 1A; skip the next (point) C of Round 3 and pass through the following C. Work 2 stitches with 1A in each stitch; pull tight. Weave through beads to exit from the second A of this round (FIG. 7, RED THREAD).

DANGLE LOOP: String 5A; pass through the A of Round 4 on the back of the bezel, directly below the current A, to form a loop. Pass back through the 5A just added and the last A exited on the front of the bezel to reinforce the loop. Weave through beads to exit from the C of Rounds 1 and 2 opposite the last A exited on the other edge of the bezel. Secure and trim the tail thread but don't trim the working thread. Set aside.

④ Assembly

Connect the components:

CONNECTION 1: Lay the large bezel and medium bezel faceup on your work surface according to FIG. 8. Use the working thread of the medium bezel to pass through the connection bead on the large bezel and the next C of Round 2 on the medium bezel (FIG. 8, PURPLE THREAD). Weave through beads to form a turnaround and pass back through the connection bead and the first C exited on the medium bezel (FIG. 8, GREEN THREAD). Secure the thread and trim.

CONNECTION 2: Lay the small bezel faceup on your work surface according to FIG. 8. Use the working thread of the small bezel to pass through the connection bead on the medium bezel and the next C of Round 2 on the small bezel (FIG. 8, BLUE THREAD). Weave through beads to form a turnaround and pass back through the connection bead and the first C exited on the small bezel (FIG. 8, RED THREAD). Secure the thread and trim.

⑤ Finish

Add the ear wire and chain fringes:

FRINGES: Cut two 1¼" (3.2cm) pieces of silver chain. Cut one 1¼" (3.2cm) piece of gunmetal chain; remove one link from the gunmetal chain so it's slightly shorter than the silver chains. Use 1 jump ring to attach one end link of each chain to the dangle loop in Step 3. *NOTE: String the chains on the jump ring in the following order: 1 silver/1 gunmetal/1 silver.*

EAR WIRE: Attach an ear wire to the ear-wire loop made in Step 1 by opening and closing the loop of the ear wire as you would a jump ring.

⑥ Repeat Steps 1–5 for a second earring, this time adding the connection beads to the right sides of the large bezel and medium bezel, the ear-wire loop to left side of the large bezel, and the dangle loop to the right side of the small bezel, so the earrings will mirror each other.

BACK OF EARRING

FIG. 8: Connecting the bezels

Equilateral

Robijo Burzynski

techniques

Circular and tubular peyote stitches

Circular and tubular herringbone stitches

materials

5 g metallic light bronze size 11° Japanese cylinder beads (A)

6 olivine 4mm crystal rounds (B)

1 pair of gold-plated 9×18mm ear wires

Smoke 6 lb FireLine braided beading thread

Beading thread wax

tools

Scissors

Size 12 beading needle

2 pairs of chain- or flat-nose pliers

FINISHED SIZE : 1⅞" (4.8cm)

❶ Inner Triangle

Use circular peyote and herringbone stitches to create the center triangle:

ROUND 1: Use 5' (1.5m) of waxed thread to string 3A; use the working and tail threads to tie a knot, leaving a 4" (10cm) tail. *NOTE: Step up for this and subsequent rounds by passing through the first A added in the current round (FIG. 1, GREEN THREAD).*

ROUND 2: String 2A and pass through the next A of Round 1; repeat twice (FIG. 1, BLUE THREAD).

ROUND 3: String 2A and pass through the next A of Round 2 to form a herringbone stitch, then string 1A and pass through the following A to form a peyote stitch; repeat twice (FIG. 1, RED THREAD).

ROUND 4: String 2A and pass through the next A of the previous round, then work 2 peyote stitches with 1A in each stitch; repeat twice (FIG. 2, GREEN THREAD).

ROUNDS 5 AND 6: Repeat Round 4 twice, increasing the number of peyote stitches along each edge by 1 stitch with each round (FIG. 2, BLUE THREAD).

ROUND 7: String 1A and pass through the next A of the previous round, then work 5 peyote stitches with 1A in each stitch; repeat twice (FIG. 2, RED THREAD). Secure and trim the tail thread. Don't trim the working thread.

❷ Outer Triangle

Use tubular peyote and herringbone stitches to form 2 layers that will be joined for the exterior triangle:

LAYER 1, ROUNDS 1 AND 2: String 1B and 1A; skip the A and pass back through the B just added and through the last A exited on the inner triangle. Pass through the 1B/1A just added. *NOTE: You'll now begin working in the opposite direction.* *String 20A and 1B; skip the next 5A of Inner Triangle, Round 7 and pass through the next (corner) A. Pass back through the B just added and through the last A strung. Pass through the nearest 1B/1A, back through the B, and through the last A strung to reinforce (FIG. 3, GREEN THREAD). Repeat from * (FIG. 3, BLUE THREAD). String 19A; pass through the first 2A of this step (FIG. 3, RED THREAD).

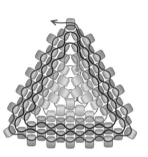

FIG. 1: Stitching Rounds 1–3 of the inner triangle

FIG. 3: Forming Layer 1, Rounds 1 and 2 of the outer triangle

FIG. 2: Working Rounds 4–7 of the inner triangle

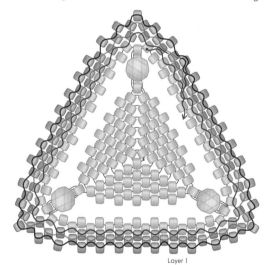

Layer 1

FIG. 4: Adding Layer 1, Rounds 3–5 of the outer triangle

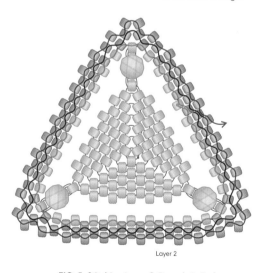

Layer 2

FIG. 5: Stitching Layer 2, Rounds 1–3 of the outer triangle

LAYER 1, ROUND 3: Work 9 peyote stitches with 1A in each stitch, then work 1 herringbone stitch with 2A, skipping the nearest corner A of Layer 1, Rounds 1 and 2; repeat twice. *NOTE: Step up for this and subsequent rounds by passing through the first A added in the current round (FIG. 4, PURPLE THREAD).*

LAYER 1, ROUND 4: Work 9 peyote stitches with 1A in each stitch, 1 herringbone stitch with 2A, and 1 peyote stitch with 1A; repeat twice (FIG. 4, GREEN THREAD).

LAYER 1, ROUND 5: Work 9 peyote stitches with 1A in each stitch, 1 stitch at the corner without skipping over any beads, and 2 peyote stitches with 1A in each stitch; repeat twice (FIG. 4, BLUE THREAD). Weave through beads to exit from 1A of Layer 1, Round 1 (FIG. 4, RED THREAD).

LAYER 2, ROUND 1: Work 30 peyote stitches off of Layer 1, Round 1 with 1A in each stitch (FIG. 5, GREEN THREAD; beads of Layer 1, Rounds 2–5 removed for clarity).

LAYER 2, ROUND 2: Work 5 peyote stitches with 1A in each stitch and 1 herringbone stitch with 2A, skipping the nearest corner A of Layer 1, Rounds 1 and 2, then work 4 peyote stitches with 1A in each stitch; repeat twice (FIG. 5, BLUE THREAD).

LAYER 2, ROUND 3: Work 5 peyote stitches with 1A in each stitch, 1 herringbone stitch with 2A, and 5 peyote stitches with 1A in each stitch; repeat twice (FIG. 5, RED THREAD).

ZIP: Pinch Layer 1 and Layer 2 together so that Layer 1, Round 5 and Layer 2, Round 3 interlock like a zipper. Weave through beads to form a seamless tube (FIG. 6; beads of Layer 1, Round 5 illustrated with an outline, and all other beads of Layer 1 removed for clarity). *NOTE: To zip the corners of the layers, pass through the first A of the corner 2A set on Layer 2, the corner A of Layer 1, then the second A of the corner 2A set on Layer 2. Weave through beads to exit from 1 corner A of the outer triangle.*

③ Ear-Wire Loop

String 6A; pass through the last A exited (FIG. 7). Repeat the thread path of this loop multiple times to reinforce. Secure the thread and trim. Attach an ear wire to the loop by opening and closing the loop of the ear wire as you would a jump ring.

④ Repeat Steps 1–3 for a second earring.

Artist's Tip

- To make a matching pendant, stitch a larger version of the triangle.

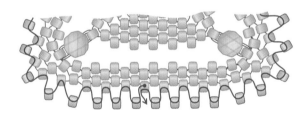

FIG. 6: Zipping Layers 1 and 2 of the outer triangle

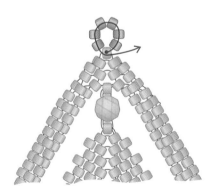

FIG. 7: Adding the ear-wire loop

variation

Embellish the exterior edge of the outer triangle with size 11° cylinder beads by stitching in the ditch.

Retro Blossom

Jill Wiseman

techniques

Tubular peyote stitch

Tubular netting

Square stitch

materials

6 g nickel-plated size 15° seed beads (A)

2 g white-lined rose size 15° seed beads (B)

8 g blue iris size 11° cylinder beads (C)

2 g periwinkle size 11° cylinder beads (D)

14 foil-back light sapphire 39ss (about 8mm) crystal chatons (E)

2 foil-back fuchsia 39ss (about 8mm) crystal chatons (F)

¾" (2cm) of sterling silver 3mm round chain

2 sterling silver 10×17mm lever-back ear wires

Smoke 6 lb braided beading thread

tools

Scissors

Size 12 beading needles

Wire cutters

FINISHED SIZE: 2¾" (7cm)

1 Bezel

Use tubular netting and peyote stitch to bezel a chaton:

ROUND 1: Use 2' (61cm) of thread to string 12C, leaving a 4" (10cm) tail; pass through all 12C again to form a tight circle. Exit through the first 1C.

ROUND 2: String 3C, skip 1C of Round 1, and pass through the next 1C to form a net; repeat five times. Step up through the first 2C added in this round (FIG. 1, BLUE THREAD).

ROUND 3: String 3A and pass through the middle 1C of the next Round 2 net; repeat five times, pulling tight so the beadwork cups. Step up through the first 2A added in this round (FIG. 1, RED THREAD).

ROUND 4: Place 1E faceup in the center of the beadwork. String 1A, 1C, and 1A and pass through the middle A of the next Round 3 net; repeat five times. Step up through the first 1A/1C added in this round (FIG. 2, BLUE THREAD).

ROUND 5: String 1A and pass through the next 1C of Round 4; repeat five times. Repeat the thread path to reinforce. Weave through beads to exit from the middle 1C of a Round 2 net (FIG. 2, RED THREAD). Secure and trim the tail thread, but leave the working thread attached. Set the bezel aside.

Repeat this entire step six times to make a total of 7 sapphire bezels. Repeat again, this time using D for C, B for A, and F for E to form 1 fuchsia bezel.

2 Connect

Use the working thread of the fuchsia bezel to square-stitch the last 1D exited in Round 2 to the middle 1C in a Round 2 net of 1 sapphire bezel. Weave through beads to exit from the middle 1D of the next Round 2 net on the fuchsia bezel. Continue square-stitching 1 sapphire bezel to each Round 2 net of the fuchsia bezel to add a total of 6 bezels (FIG. 3, BLUE THREAD). Secure the fuchsia bezel's thread and trim.

Use the working thread of the sapphire bezels to square-stitch the touching 1Cs of Round 2, forming 6 more connections (FIG. 3, RED THREAD). Secure 5 of the threads and trim. Weave the remaining thread through beads to exit from a sapphire bezel's outermost middle 1C of Round 2.

3 Assembly

Add the upper bezel, chain, and ear wire to complete the earring:

CHAIN BOTTOM: String 1A, one end of one ⅜" (1cm) piece of chain, and 1A, then pass through the last 1C exited on the bezel; repeat the thread path to reinforce (FIG. 4, GREEN THREAD). Secure the thread and trim.

CHAIN TOP: Use the working thread of the remaining sapphire bezel to string 1A, the free end of the chain, and 1A, then pass through the last 1C exited on the bezel; repeat the thread path to reinforce. Weave through beads to exit from the middle 1C of the Round 2 net on the other side of the bezel (FIG. 4, BLUE THREAD).

EAR WIRE: String 2A, the loop of an ear wire, and 2A, then pass through the last 1C exited; repeat the thread path to reinforce (FIG. 4, RED THREAD). Secure the thread and trim.

4 Repeat Steps 1–3 for a second earring.

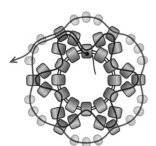

FIG. 1: Forming Rounds 2 and 3 of the bezel

FIG. 2: Working Rounds 4 and 5

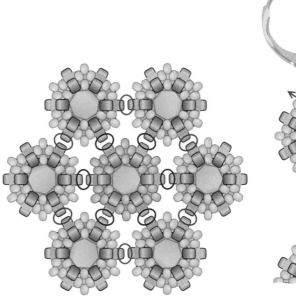

FIG. 3: Connecting the bezels

FIG. 4: Assembling the earring

Desert Thistle

Kristen Winter

techniques

Circular brick stitch

Circular herringbone stitch

Picot

materials

2 g bronze-lined clear size 8° seed beads (A)

1 g metallic antique gold size 8° seed beads (B)

2 g transparent amethyst size 8° cylinder beads (C)

2 g brown iris size 6° seed beads (D)

2 g bronze-lined black diamond AB 3mm triangles (E)

2 copper 13mm (outside diameter)/8mm (inside diameter) hammered seamless flat rings

1 pair of bronze ¾" (2cm) ear wires

Brown size D nylon beading thread

tools

Scissors

Beading needle

FINISHED SIZE: 2¼" (5.5cm)

① Body

Use circular brick and herringbone stitches to form the body of the earring, then add picots:

ROUND 1: Tie the end of 6' (1.8m) of thread to 1 ring, leaving a 6" (15cm) tail. String 2E; pass through the ring and back through the second E so the beads sit on the outside of the ring (FIG. 1, BLUE THREAD). String 1E, pass through the ring, and back through the E just added (FIG. 1, RED THREAD); repeat fourteen times for a total of 17E or until the E completely surround the ring. Pass down through the first E added in this round, through the ring, and back through the first E (FIG. 2).

ROUND 2: String 2D; skip one thread between beads (this is called a "thread bridge") in Round 1, pass under the next thread bridge, and pass back through the second D (FIG. 3, BLUE THREAD). String 1D, pass under the next thread bridge between the following 2E of Round 1, and back through the D just added (FIG. 3, RED THREAD); repeat fourteen times for a total of 17D. Pass down through the first D added in this round, under the next thread bridge, and back through the first D. *NOTE: To fit the larger D beads over the smaller E, you will need to decide which will be the best thread bridge to pass under, sometimes skipping thread bridges in order to keep the work even and tight.*

ROUND 3: Work 28 brick stitches with 1A in each stitch or an even number that fits evenly around Round 2. Pass down through the first A added in this round, under the next thread bridge, and back through the first A. *NOTE: To fit the smaller A over the larger D, it will be necessary to brick-stitch into some of the thread bridges more than once.*

ROUND 4: String 2C, pass down through the next A in Round 3, and up through the following A; repeat thirteen times for a total of 14 herringbone stitches (FIG. 4, GREEN THREAD). Step up through the first C added in this round.

ROUND 5: String 1A, 1B, and 1A; pass down through the next C in Round 4 and up through the following C; repeat thirteen times for a total of 14 picots (FIG. 4, BLUE THREAD). Weave through beads to exit from 1B.

② Loop

String 2B, an ear wire, and 2B; pass through the last B exited to form a loop (FIG. 4, RED THREAD). Repeat the thread path several times to reinforce. Secure the threads and trim.

③ Repeat Steps 1 and 2 for a second earring.

FIG. 1: Beginning Round 1

FIG. 2: Forming the last stitch of Round 1

FIG. 3: Adding the first 2 stitches of Round 2

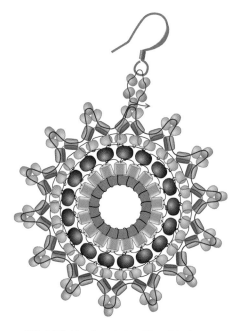

FIG. 4: Stitching Rounds 4 and 5 and the loop

Tundra

Debora Hodoyer

techniques

Circular peyote stitch

Circular herringbone stitch

Picot

Netting

materials

12 matte starlight galvanized size 15°
seed beads (A)

1 g matte dark copper size 11° seed
beads (B)

1.5 g matte metallic brass gold 3.8×1mm
O beads (C)

4.5 g metallic olive 5×2.5mm 2-hole
SuperDuos (D)

16 milky white-and-caramel luster
3×2mm crystal rondelles (E)

8 carnation pink luster 4mm fire-polished
rounds (F)

2 light rose 8mm pearl rounds (G)

1 pair of gold-plated 13×27mm ear wires

Beige size D nylon beading thread

tools

Scissors

Size 12 beading needle

2 pairs of chain- or flat-nose
pliers

FINISHED SIZE: 2¼" (5.5cm)

1 Earring

Use circular peyote and herringbone stitches, picots, and netting to create the earring:

ROUND 1: Use 4' (10cm) of thread to string 8D, leaving a 6" (15cm) tail; pass through all the beads again to form a tight circle and use the working and tail threads to tie a knot. Step up through the second (outside) hole of the first D added (FIG. 1).

ROUND 2: String 1D and pass through the next D (outside hole) of the previous round; repeat seven times. Step up through the outside hole of the first D added in this round (FIG. 2, BLUE THREAD).

ROUND 3: Repeat Round 2 (FIG. 2, RED THREAD).

CENTER: String 1G; skip 3D of Round 3 and pass through the fourth D (outside hole) of Round 3, opposite the last D exited. Pass back through the G and through the first D (outside hole) exited in this round (FIG. 3, BLUE THREAD). *NOTE: Rounds 2 and 3 will fold up and around the G, so the outside holes of the D in Round 3 will touch the G.*

ROUND 4: String 1E and pass through the next D (through the hole nearest the G) of Round 3; repeat seven times. Repeat the thread path to reinforce; pass back through the second hole (the hole farthest from the G) of the current D (FIG. 3, RED THREAD). *NOTE: You will now begin stitching in the opposite direction.*

ROUND 5: String 1C, 2D, and 1C; pass back through the next D (through the hole on the outside edge of the beadwork) of Round 3 (FIG. 4, GREEN THREAD). String 1B, 1F, and 1B; pass back through the next D (through the hole on the outside edge of the beadwork) of Round 3 (FIG. 4, BLUE THREAD). Repeat from the beginning of this round three times. Pass through the first 1C and the second (outside) hole of the first D added in this round (FIG. 4, RED THREAD).

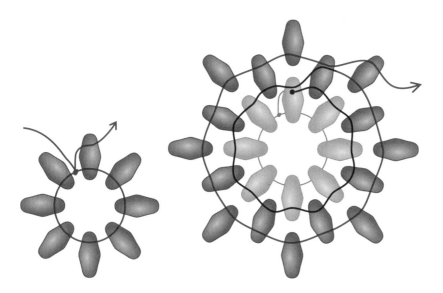

FIG. 1: Forming Round 1

FIG. 2: Stitching Rounds 2 and 3

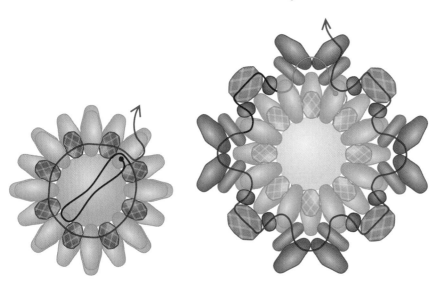

FIG. 3: Adding the center bead and Round 4

FIG. 4: Working Round 5

ROUND 6: String 1D and 3B; pass through the second hole of the D just added. Pass through the following D (outside hole) of Round 5 (FIG. 5, PURPLE THREAD). String 2B; pass through the nearest F of Round 5. String 2B; pass through the next D (outside hole) of Round 5 (FIG. 5, GREEN THREAD). Repeat from the beginning of this round three times. Pass through the first 1D (right hole)/2B added in this round (FIG. 5, BLUE THREAD).

EAR WIRE: String 3A, an ear wire, and 3A and pass through the last B exited; repeat the thread path several times to reinforce. Weave through beads to exit from the first F of Round 5 (FIG. 5, RED THREAD).

ROUND 7: String 1C, 1B, 1C, 1B, and 1C; pass through the last F exited. Weave through the beads of Rounds 5 and 6 to exit from the next F of Round 5 (FIG. 6, GREEN THREAD). Repeat from the beginning of this round three times, exiting from the first B of the 2B set of Round 6 before the next F of Round 5 (FIG. 6, BLUE THREAD).

ROUND 8: String 1B; pass through the next 1C/1B/1C/1B/1C of Round 7. String 1B; weave through beads to exit from the first B of the 2B set of Round 6 before the next F of Round 5. Repeat from the beginning of this round three times (FIG. 6, RED THREAD). Secure the threads and trim them.

2 Repeat Step 1 for a second earring.

Artist's Tip

- Work with a medium-high tension and use your fingers to keep the beads firmly in position while you pull the thread.

FIG. 5: Stitching Round 6 and adding the ear wire

FIG. 6: Adding Rounds 7 and 8

Season's Delights

Alice Kharon

techniques

Right-angle weave

Peyote stitch

materials

1 g gold metallic size 15° seed beads (A)

1 g turquoise-lined clear size 15° seed beads (B)

1 g dark gold luster size 11° seed beads (C)

54 dark bronze 3mm fire-polished rounds (D)

18 coral 3mm crystal pearls (E)

2 white 12mm crystal pearls (F)

2 gold 5mm closed (soldered) jump rings

1 pair of gold ½" (1.3cm) ear wires

Smoke 6 lb braided beading thread

tools

Size 12 beading needle

Scissors or thread burner

2 pairs of chain- or flat-nose pliers

FINISHED SIZE: 1½" (3.8cm)

① Band

Weave and embellish a right-angle-weave band to encircle a 12mm pearl:

ROUND 1, UNIT 1: Use 3' (91.5cm) of thread to string 4D, leaving a 3" (7.5cm) tail. Tie the working and tail threads together to form a tight circle, pass through the beads again to hide the tail, pass through the first 3D, and trim the tail.

ROUND 1, UNITS 2–9: String 3D, pass through the last D exited and the first 2D just strung; repeat seven times.

ROUND 1, UNIT 10: String 1D; pass through the end D in Unit 1. String 1D; pass through the end D in Unit 9, pulling tight to form a ring. Weave through beads to exit from a side D of one of the right-angle-weave units (FIG. 1).

CENTER PEARL: String 1F, pass through the D on the opposite side of the ring, pass back through the F, the D originally exited, and the top D of the nearest unit (FIG. 2).

ROUND 2: String 1A, 1E, and 1A, pass through the bottom D of the same unit, and weave through beads to exit from the top D of the next unit (FIG. 3); repeat eight times to embellish each right-angle-weave unit with a diagonal strand. Weave through beads to exit an edge D from Round 1.

ROUND 3: *String 1B and pass through the top D of the next unit; repeat around to add a total of 9B. Weave through beads to exit from a bottom D at the other edge of the ring and repeat from *, this time adding 1B between each bottom D. Exit from a side D of Round 1 (FIG. 4).

② Loop

String 7A and 1 jump ring; pass through the last D exited to form a loop (FIG. 5). Repeat the thread path several times to reinforce; secure the thread and trim. Connect an ear wire to the jump ring.

③ Repeat Steps 1 and 2 to form the second earring.

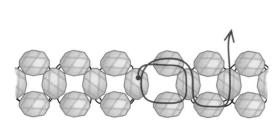

FIG. 1: Turning the right-angle-weave band into a ring

FIG. 2: Stringing the focal bead

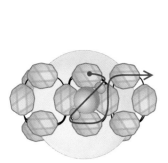

FIG. 3: Adding the first stitch of Round 2

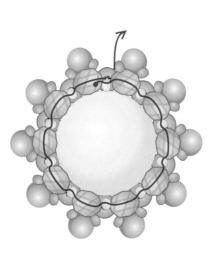

FIG. 4: Stitching the second side of Round 3

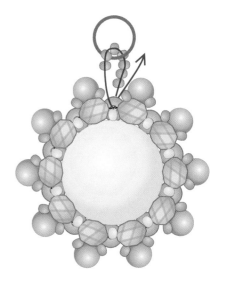

FIG. 5: Adding the loop

Parthenope

Maggie Meister

techniques
Circular and tubular peyote stitch

Ladder stitch

Tubular herringbone stitch

Square stitch

Picot

materials
5 g 24k gold-plated size 15° seed
beads (A)

5 g matte 24k gold-plated size 11° cylinder
beads (B)

14 cream 3mm pearls (C)

2 ruby 12mm top-drilled coins

1 pair of gold-filled ⅝" (1.5cm) lever-back
ear wires

Gold size D nylon beading thread

Double-sided craft tape

tools
Scissors

Size 12 beading needle

Size 12 sharp needle

FINISHED SIZE: 2⅛" (5.4cm)

❶ Bezel

Work circular and tubular peyote stitch to bezel a ruby coin:

ROUND 1: Use 6' (1.8m) of thread and a beading needle to string 3B, leaving a 4" (10cm) tail. Pass through all the beads again to form a tight circle, then pass through the first B strung.

ROUND 2: String 1B and pass through the next B of Round 1; repeat twice. Unless otherwise noted, step up through the first bead added in this and subsequent rounds (FIG. 1, PURPLE THREAD).

ROUND 3: Work 3 stitches with 2B in each stitch (FIG. 1, ORANGE THREAD).

ROUND 4: Work 6 stitches with 1B in each stitch, splitting the pairs of the previous round (FIG. 1, GREEN THREAD).

ROUND 5: Work 6 stitches with 2B in each stitch (FIG. 1, BLUE THREAD).

ROUND 6: Work 12 stitches with 1B in each stitch (FIG. 1, RED THREAD).

RUBY: Place a small amount of tape on the back of 1 coin, taking care it doesn't overlap the edges. Peel the paper backing off of the tape, if needed, and attach the coin to the beadwork so the coin's hole sits near the last B exited. Pass through the coin, into the nearest B on the other end of the coin's hole, back through the coin, and through the first B exited (FIG. 2).

ROUND 7: Work 12 stitches with 1B in each stitch (FIG. 3, PURPLE THREAD).

ROUND 8: Work 1 stitch with 1B, then 1 stitch with 2B; repeat five times (FIG. 3, ORANGE THREAD).

ROUND 9: Work 12 stitches with 1B in each stitch, treating each 2B stitch of Round 8 as 1 bead (FIG. 3, GREEN THREAD).

ROUND 10: Work 1 stitch with 2B, then 1 stitch with 1B; repeat five times. Step up through the first 2B added in this round (FIG. 3, BLUE THREAD). *NOTE: At this point, the sides of the ruby should be covered with beads and the ruby should be held firmly in place. If not, repeat Round 9 until the ruby is covered.*

ROUND 11: Work 12 stitches with 1A in each stitch, treating each 2B stitch of Round 10 as 1 bead (FIG. 3, RED THREAD). Secure the thread and trim.

❷ Rope

Work tubular herringbone stitch to form the rope that will surround the bezel:

ROUND 1: Use 6' (1.8m) of thread and a beading needle to ladder-stitch a strip 4A long, leaving a 6" (15cm) tail. Taking care that the strip isn't twisted, square-stitch the first and last A together to form a ring (FIG. 4, BLUE THREAD).

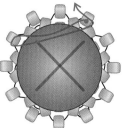

FIG. 1: Forming Rounds 2–6 of the bezel

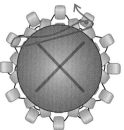

FIG. 2: Setting the ruby

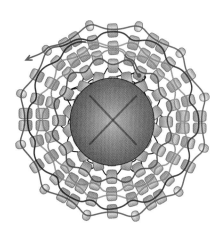

FIG. 3: Stitching Rounds 7–11 of the bezel

FIG. 4: Forming Rounds 1 and 2 of the rope

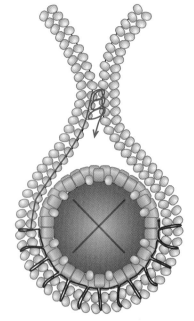

FIG. 5: Connecting the rope to the bezel

ROUND 2: String 2A, then pass down through the next A of the previous round and up through the following A; repeat. Step up through the first A added in this round (FIG. 4, RED THREAD).

ROUND 3 AND ON: Repeat Round 2 until the rope is 3½" (9cm) long. Use a ladder-stitch thread path to close the last round. Don't trim the thread; set aside.

③ Assembly

Connect the rope to the bezel, embellish, and finish:

FIG. 6: Curving and embellishing the earring

ROPE-BEZEL CONNECTION: Using a sharp needle, start 2' (61cm) of new thread that exits from Round 8 of the bezel. Wrap the rope around the bezel so the rope ends are paired up at the top and the bezel thread exits from the three o'clock position. Pass straight through the rope, over the thread on the rope to catch it, back through the rope, and through the next 1B or 2B in Round 8 of the bezel. Continue connecting the rope to the bezel in the same way so the entire bottom half of the bezel (from three o'clock to nine o'clock) is firmly attached to the rope (FIG. 5, BLUE THREAD).

CENTER CURVE: Weave through beads to exit from the eleventh round from one end of 1 rope, from an A at the center where the ropes will touch. Square-stitch this A to the mirror A on the other end of the rope; repeat twice to connect Rounds 12 and 13 on the inside, touching edges of the rope ends (FIG. 5, RED THREAD). Then work up the back of the ropes to join the remaining column of unconnected beads on the inside edge.

Artist's Tip

- Center-drilled coins would also work for the bezels; be sure to stitch them over the center of the beadwork after Round 6.

RIGHT TOP CURVE: Weave through beads to exit up through an outside Round 2 bead of the right rope end. String 1A and catch the thread on the outside of the rope that connects the beads of the next round; repeat six times to embellish the outer edge of the rope with a total of 7A. Pull tightly so the rope curves outward to the right (FIG. 6, ORANGE THREAD). Tie a half-hitch knot between beads to hold the curve in place.

BOTTOM EMBELLISHMENT: String 1A, 1C, and 1A; skip 4A of the rope and pass through the next A to form a picot. Weave through beads to add matching picots on the outside of the rope at the three, six, and nine o'clock positions around the bezel and on the mirror point from the first embellishment, but only skip 2A of the rope when stitching the 3 picots around the bezel (FIG. 6, GREEN THREAD).

LEFT TOP CURVE: Repeat the right top curve, this time moving from bottom to top and pulling tightly so the rope curves outward to the left (FIG. 6, BLUE THREAD).

TOP EMBELLISHMENTS AND EAR WIRE: Exiting up through the left side of the left rope end, string 1A, 1C, and 1A; pass down through the right side of the left rope end and exit down through Round 4. String 4A, an ear wire, and 4A; catch a thread above Round 5 on the left side of the right rope end. Pass back through the 4A/ear wire/4A to reinforce, catch a thread on the mirror side of the rope, and pass through the 4A/ear wire/4A again. Pass up through the 4 end rounds on the left side of the right rope. String 1A, 1C, and 1A; pass down through the right side of the right rope end (FIG. 6, RED THREAD). Secure the thread and trim.

④ Repeat Steps 1–3 for a second earring.

Royal Amethyst

Cecilia Guastaferro

techniques
Two-needle right-angle weave

Wireworking

materials
5 g antiqued gold metallic size 11° cylinder beads

32 clear 3mm fire-polished rounds

2 amethyst 6×9mm faceted glass teardrops

32 ivory 2mm glass pearls

2 amethyst 13×18mm cabochons

2 antiqued brass 5×2mm flower bead caps

2 antiqued brass 2" (5cm) head pins

2 antiqued brass 4mm jump rings

1 pair of antiqued brass lever-back ear wires

Clear .010 monofilament cord

G-S Hypo Cement

tools
Scissors

Big-eye needles (optional)

FINISHED SIZE: 1¾" (4.5cm)

❶ Bezel

Use cylinder, clear round, and pearl beads to form a two-needle right-angle-weave bezel for the cabochon:

ROUND 1: Use 2' (61cm) of cord to string 32 cylinder beads (a needle is not necessary). Slide the beads to the center of the cord. Pass through the first bead strung to form a circle.

ROUND 2: Use the right cord to string 1 cylinder bead, 1 pearl, and 1 cylinder bead; skip the next Round 1 cylinder bead to the left and pass through the following cylinder bead (FIG. 1, RED THREAD). Pass the left cord back through the last cylinder bead strung (FIG. 1, BLUE THREAD). *Use what is now the right cord to string 1 pearl and 1 cylinder bead; skip the next Round 1 cylinder bead and pass through the following one. Pass the left cord back through the last cylinder bead strung. Repeat from * to work a round of right-angle weave. To close the round and step up to the next, string 1 pearl on the right cord and pass the left cord through the first cylinder bead added in this step and back through the pearl just strung (FIG. 2).

ROUND 3: Use the right cord to string 1 clear round, 1 cylinder bead, and 1 clear round and pass through the next Round 2 pearl to the left. Pass the left cord back through the last clear round strung. *Use what is now the right cord to string 1 cylinder bead and 1 clear round; pass through the next Round 2 pearl. Pass the left cord back through the last clear round strung. Repeat from * to work a round of right-angle weave. To close the round and step up to the next, string 1 cylinder bead on the right cord and pass the left cord through the first clear round added in this step and back through the cylinder bead just added (FIG. 3).

ROUND 4: Work another round of two-needle right-angle weave using all cylinder beads. Before closing the round, place 1 cabochon inside the beadwork so its face touches Round 1. Pass both cords through a final cylinder bead in opposite directions and pull the cord very tight. Weave the working cords through the up beads of this round again in opposite directions.

When they meet again, pull the cord very tight and tie a square knot (Fig. 4). Apply cement on the knot, allow to dry, and trim thread.

❷ Loops

Pass 10" (25.5cm) of cord through the clear round at the top of the cabochon, leaving a 4" (10cm) tail. String 5 cylinder beads and pass through the clear round again (FIG. 5). Repeat the thread path several times. Secure the cord, glue the knot, allow to dry, and trim. Repeat to add a loop to the bottom of the cabochon. Attach 1 loop to an ear wire using 1 jump ring.

❸ Dangle

Use 1 head pin to string 1 bead cap and 1 teardrop. Form a wrapped loop that attaches to the cabochon's other loop.

❹ Repeat Steps 1–3 for a second earring.

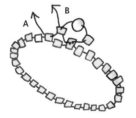

FIG. 1: Starting Round 2

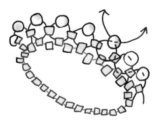

FIG. 2: Finishing Round 2

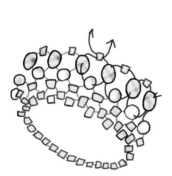

FIG. 3: Stitching Round 3

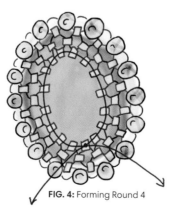

FIG. 4: Forming Round 4

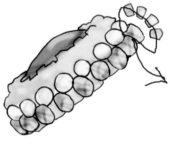

FIG. 5: Forming the loop

Flamenco Flourish

Svetlana Chernitsky

techniques

Two-needle right-angle weave variation

Peyote stitch

materials

0.5 g metallic gold iris size 15° Japanese seed beads (A)

0.5 g metallic gold iris size 11° Japanese seed beads (B)

3 g brown iris 5×2.5mm 2-hole seed beads (C)

4 crystal dorado 2X 3mm crystal bicones (D)

12 crystal dorado 2X 4mm crystal bicones (E)

2 jet sliperit 12mm 2-hole bead studs (F)

2 marea peacock–coated gold 5×16mm
    2-hole pressed-glass daggers (G)

24 hybrid magic orchid 3.4mm Japanese drops (H)

1 pair of antiqued brass 10×15mm lever-back ear wires

Smoke 6 lb braided beading thread

tools

Scissors

Size 12 beading needles

FINISHED SIZE: 2⅝" (6.7cm)

① Base

Use a variation of two-needle right-angle weave to form the earring base:

UNIT 1: Place a needle at each end of 3' (91.5cm) of thread. Use one needle to string 1E, 1B, 3C, 1B, 1G (top hole), 1B, 3C, and 1B. Move the beads to the center of the thread; repeat the thread path twice to reinforce and form a circle. Pass through 1E (FIG. 1). *NOTE: Because of the nature of this project, the needle will switch left and right positions with each unit.*

UNIT 2: Use the right needle to string 1B, 1E, 1B, and 1C, then pass through the second hole of the same C (FIG. 2, GREEN THREAD); repeat using the left needle. Continuing with the left needle, string 1F (bottom hole) and pass back through the first C (top hole) added in this unit (FIG. 2, BLUE THREAD). Use the right needle to pass back through the F (bottom hole) and the following C (top hole) (FIG. 2, RED THREAD).

UNIT 3: Use the right needle to string 4C; pass through the F (top hole) (FIG. 3, GREEN THREAD). Use the left needle to string 4C; pass back through the F (top hole) and the nearest C (inside hole). Pass through the outside hole of the same C (FIG. 3, BLUE THREAD). Use the right needle (now exiting the left side of the F) to pass through the nearest 5C (inside holes), the F (bottom hole), 5C (inside holes), the F (top hole), and inside and outside holes of the next C (FIG. 3, RED THREAD).

UNIT 4: Use the right needle to string 1B, 1E, 1B, and 1E (FIG. 4, BLUE THREAD). Use the left needle to string 1B, 1E, and 1B; pass back through the last E added in this unit (FIG. 4, RED THREAD).

② Ear Wire

Use the right needle to string 4A, an ear wire, and 4A; pass through the last E exited to form a loop (FIG. 5, BLUE THREAD). Use the left needle to pass back through 4A, the ear wire, 4A, and current 1E to reinforce the stitch (FIG. 5, RED THREAD).

③ Embellishment

Finish the sides of the earring with peyote stitch:

PASS 1: Using the right needle, pass through the nearest 1B/1E/1B/1C (outside hole). String 1H and pass through the following C (outside hole); repeat three times (FIG. 6, PURPLE THREAD). Pass through the nearest 1B/1E/1B/1E/1B and the outside hole of the following C. String 1H and pass through the following C (outside hole); repeat (FIG. 6, GREEN THREAD). String 1A, 1D, and 1A; pass through the bottom hole of the G (FIG. 6, BLUE THREAD).

FIG. 1: Forming Unit 1 of the base

FIG. 2: Adding Unit 2 of the base

FIG. 3: Completing Unit 3 of the base

PASS 2: Use the left needle to repeat Pass 1 on the opposite side of the beadwork (FIG. 6, RED THREAD). Secure the threads and trim.

4 Repeat Steps 1–3 for a second earring.

FIG. 4: Forming Unit 4 of the base

FIG. 5: Adding the ear wire

FIG. 6: Adding the embellishment

Ruby Ripples

Sandie Bachand

techniques

Circular square stitch

Circular right-angle weave

Fringe

materials

1 g silver size 15° seed beads (A)

2 ruby 8mm crystal bicones

44 magenta 2mm glass pearl rounds (B)

44 silver-plated 2.5mm cornerless cubes (C)

2 silver-plated 15mm coins with crystal and magenta rhinestone inlay

2 silver-plated 8×15mm ear wires

Smoke 6 lb braided beading thread

tools

Scissors

Size 12 beading needle

FINISHED SIZE: 2¼" (5.5cm)

1 Body

Use circular square stitch and circular right-angle weave to form the body of the earring:

ROUND 1: Use 6' (1.8m) of thread to string 42A, leaving a 6" (15cm) tail. Wrap the beads around the circumference of the coin; use the working and tail threads to tie a secure knot. String the coin and pass through the nearest 2A (FIG. 1).

ROUND 2: String 1C, then pass through the last 2A exited in the previous round and the next 2A (FIG. 2, BLUE THREAD); repeat twenty times for a total of 21C. Pass back through the nearest C of this round (FIG. 2, RED THREAD).

ROUND 3, UNIT 1: String 1A, 1B, and 1A; pass through the last C exited in Round 2 and up through the first A just added (FIG. 3, PINK THREAD). *NOTE: When working the right-angle-weave units, be sure to keep the seed beads from sliding down the thread and into the holes of the cornerless cubes.*

ROUND 3, UNIT 2: String 1B and 1A; pass back through the next C of Round 2, up through the nearest side A of the previous unit, through the 1B/1A just added, and back through the next C of Round 2 (FIG. 3, ORANGE THREAD).

ROUND 3, UNIT 3: String 1A and 1B; pass down through the nearest side A of the previous unit, through the last C exited from Round 2, and up through the first A just added (FIG. 3, PURPLE THREAD).

ROUND 3, UNITS 4-21: Repeat Round 3, Units 2 and 3, eight times, then repeat Unit 2 (FIG. 3, GREEN THREAD). Pass up through the nearest side A of Round 3, Unit 1. String 1B; pass down through the nearest side A of Unit 20, through the last C exited from Round 2, and up through the nearest side A of Unit 1 (FIG. 3, BLUE THREAD). Weave through beads to exit from 1B at the top of the beadwork (FIG. 3, RED THREAD).

2 Ear Wire

String 1B, 5A, and an ear wire; pass back through the B just added and through the next B on the edge of the beadwork. Weave through beads and repeat the thread path to reinforce. Weave through beads to exit from 1B at the bottom of the beadwork (FIG. 4, BLUE THREAD).

3 Dangle

String 1C, 1 crystal, and 1A; pass back through the crystal/1C and the last B exited. Repeat the thread path to reinforce (FIG. 4, RED THREAD). Secure the thread and trim.

4 Repeat Steps 1–3 for a second earring.

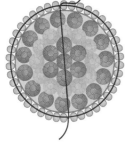

FIG. 1: Forming Round 1 of the earring body

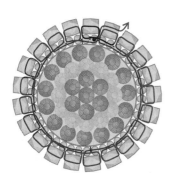

FIG. 2: Adding Round 2 of the body

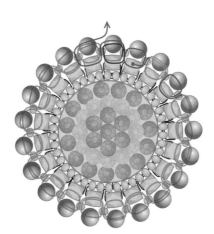

FIG. 3: Working Round 3 of the body

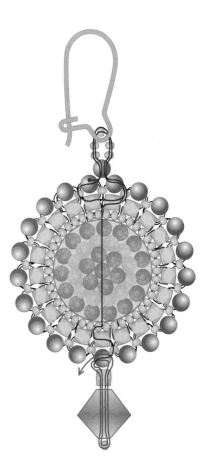

FIG. 4: Attaching the ear wire and adding the dangle

MAIN COLORWAY

Sundial

Breanna Garcia

techniques

Right-angle weave variation

Circular peyote stitch

materials

0.5 g rose gold size 15° seed beads (A)

0.5 g matte jet size 15° seed beads (B)

0.5 g rose gold size 11° seed beads (C)

0.5 g matte jet size 11° seed beads (D)

1 g jet Capri gold 4×5mm dragon scale beads (E)

2 copper ombré polychrome 8mm 2-hole Tipp beads (F)

1 pair of sterling silver 6mm flat-pad ear studs (with earring backs)

Black 10 lb WildFire thermally bonded beading thread

Clear craft adhesive

tools

Scissors or thread zapper (optional)

Size 12 beading needle

FINISHED SIZE: 1 1/16" (1.7cm)

① Bezel Front

Use a variation of right-angle weave to stitch the front of the bezel:

UNIT 1: *NOTE: The Capri gold dragon scale beads (E) are gold on one side and jet on the other. Orient 2E on your work surface with the gold sides faceup; these will be referred to as "gold E." Orient 8E on your work surface with the jet side faceup; these will be referred to as "jet E."* Use 2' (61cm) of thread to string 1C, 1 gold E, 1C, and 1 jet E, leaving an 8" (20.5cm) tail (FIG. 1, TURQUOISE THREAD). Pass through the beads again to form a tight circle and exit from the first C; the gold side of each E should face the front. Hold the beadwork in your nondominant hand with the gold sides of each E facing you. *NOTE: With each subsequent unit, maintain tight tension and position the scales so the pointed end without a hole faces out.*

UNIT 2: String 1A, 1C, 1 gold E, and 1C; pass through the nearest E of the previous unit from back to front. Repeat the thread path of this unit, skipping the A and exiting from the first C (FIG. 1, PURPLE THREAD).

UNIT 3: String 1A, 1D, 1 jet E, and 1D; pass through the nearest E of the previous unit from back to front. Repeat the thread path of this unit, skipping the last A added and exiting from the first D (FIG. 1, GREEN THREAD).

UNITS 4–9: Repeat Round 1, Unit 3 six times, using B for A (FIG. 1, YELLOW THREAD).

UNIT 10 (JOIN): String 1B and 1D; pass through the nearest E of Round 1, Unit 1 from front to back. String 1D; pass through the last E added in Round 1, Unit 9 from back to front. Repeat the thread path of this unit to reinforce, skipping the last B added and exiting from the first D. String 1A; pass through the nearest C and the following E from front to back (FIG. 1, RED THREAD). Flip the beadwork over so the back is faceup. *NOTE: The colors of the beads will switch in the following illustration because of the finish on the beads.*

FIG. 1: Stitching the bezel front

FIG. 2: Adding the center

FIG. 3: Finishing the bezel back

② Center

Add a Tipp bead to the center of the bezel:

CONNECTION 1: Holding 1F with the point facedown, string the left hole of the F and pass down through the fourth E to the left of the last E exited. Pass back through the left hole of the F and pass up through the first E exited in this step, the next C, and the following E (FIG. 2, BLUE THREAD).

CONNECTION 2: Pass through the right hole of the F and pass down through the fourth E to the right of the last E exited. Pass back through the right hole of the F and pass up through the first E exited in this step and the next C (FIG. 2, RED THREAD).

③ Bezel Back

String 1A; pass through the next C (FIG. 3, PURPLE THREAD). String 1A; pass through the next D (FIG. 3, GREEN THREAD). String 1B and pass through the next D; repeat six times (FIG. 3, BLUE THREAD). String 1A; pass through the next C (FIG. 3, RED THREAD). Repeat the thread path of this round to reinforce. Secure and trim the working thread.

④ Front Reinforcement

Use the tail thread to pass through all the seed beads at the front of the bezel. Secure and trim the tail thread.

⑤ Finish

Apply a small amount of adhesive to the pad of the earring post and adhere it to the back of the F; let dry.

⑥ Repeat Steps 1–5 for a second earring.

Artist's Tips

- When adding the dragon scale beads, make sure they are pointing upward before you tighten the stitch.

- When working Round 1 of the bezel front, double-check that the thread doesn't get caught on the size 15° seed bead of each unit that you skip when tightening the stitch.

- You can use a 7mm two-hole cabochon instead of a Tipp bead; you'll only need 9E around it rather than 10.

- A thread zapper works better than scissors for finishing WildFire thread.

MAIN COLORWAY

Drop-Dead Gorgeous

Tina Häuer

techniques

Tubular and odd-count flat peyote stitch

materials

1 g metallic silver size 15° seed beads (A)

1 g metallic gold size 15° seed beads (B)

2 g matte metallic silver size 11° cylinder beads (C)

2 metallic silver 2x4mm glass drops

2 foil-back purple/blue 16mm crystal rivolis

1 pair of gold ½" (1.3cm) ear wires

Smoke 6 lb braided beading thread

tools

Scissors or thread burner

Size 13 beading needles

2 pairs of chain- or flat-nose pliers

FINISHED SIZE: 1⅝" (4.1cm)

❶ Bezel

Use tubular peyote stitch to bezel the rivoli:

ROUNDS 1 AND 2: Use 3' (91.5cm) of thread to string 40C, leaving a 2" (5cm) tail. Tie a knot to form a circle and pass through the first 2C.

ROUND 3: String 1C, skip 1C of the starting circle, and pass through the next C; repeat to add a total of 20C. Step up for the next and subsequent rounds by passing through the first bead added in the current round.

ROUNDS 4 AND 5: Work 20 stitches with 1C in each stitch for a total of 2 rounds. Check to see if the rivoli will fit inside the beadwork. If it's too tight, stretch the beadwork a bit to make it fit. If it's too loose, work with tighter tension.

ROUNDS 6 AND 7: Work 20 stitches with 1A in each stitch for a total of 2 rounds. Weave through beads to exit from Round 1. Secure the tail thread and trim.

ROUNDS 8 AND 9: Place the rivoli in the beadwork so the back touches Round 7. Work 20 stitches with 1B in each stitch for a total of 2 rounds, pulling the rounds tight to bezel the rivoli. Weave through beads to exit from Round 3 (FIG. 1).

❷ Point

Use odd-count flat peyote stitch for a decorative point on the bezel:

ROW 1: String 1C and pass through the next C of Round 3; repeat four times for a total of 5C. Step up for the next row by weaving through the beads of Rounds 2 and 4 to pass back through the last C added (FIG. 2). *NOTE: Use pliers to carefully pull the needle and thread through beads if necessary.*

ROW 2: Work 4 stitches with 1C in each stitch. Loop the thread between the next 2C; pass back through the first C added in the previous row and the final C added in the current row to form a turnaround (FIG. 3).

ROW 3: Work 3 stitches with 1C in each stitch; form a turnaround as in Row 2. *NOTE: Keep the thread tension tight so that the beadwork curves down and away from the front of the rivoli.*

ROW 4: Work 2 stitches with 1C in each stitch; form a turnaround as in Row 2.

ROW 5: Work 1 stitch with 1 drop. Form a turnaround as in Row 2 and reinforce the stitch (FIG. 4). Weave through beads to exit from the C in Round 3 of the bezel opposite the center of the point just formed.

❸ Loop

String 10B and pass through the last C exited to form a loop (FIG. 5). Repeat the thread path to reinforce. Secure the thread and trim. Connect an ear wire to the loop using the pliers.

❹ Repeat Steps 1–3 to form the second earring.

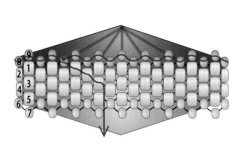

FIG. 1: Stitching Rounds 1–9 of the bezel

FIG. 2: Stepping up for Row 2

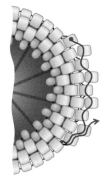

FIG. 3: Adding Row 2

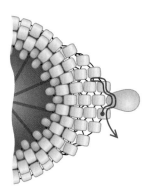

FIG. 4: Completing the point

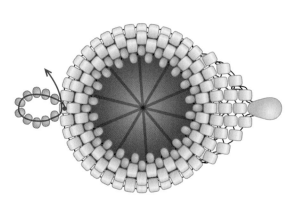

FIG. 5: Adding the loop

Ice Drop

Linda McKee

techniques

Circular brick stitch

Netting

Stringing

materials

3 g turquoise size 11° seed beads (A)

26 silver 5×2.5mm 2-hole seed beads (B)

12 turquoise 3mm fire-polished rounds (C)

2 teal 6mm fire-polished rounds (D)

12 indicolite 4mm crystal bicones (E)

2 white 12mm crystal pearl rounds (F)

2 silver 10×20mm ear wires

Crystal 6 lb braided beading thread

Thread conditioner

tools

Scissors

Size 11 beading needle

FINISHED SIZE: 2¼" (5.5cm)

❶ Earring

Stitch the body of the earring:

BASE: Use 3' (91.5 cm) of thread to string 1F, leaving a 4" (10 cm) tail. Pass through the F; repeat three times. Arrange the threads to form 2 sets of 2 base threads on each side of the F (FIG. 1).

ROUND 1: String 2A; pass under the set of 2 base threads, and pass back through the second A just strung. String 1A, pass under the base threads, and pass back through the A just strung; repeat seventeen times for a total of 20A. Pass down through the first A of this round and up through the last A added (FIG. 2).

ROUND 2: String 1A, 2B, and 1A; skip 1A of Round 1, then pass down through the next A and up through the following A (FIG. 3, ORANGE THREAD). String 1A, 1B, and 1A, then skip 1A of Round 1, pass down through the next A and up through the following A; repeat (FIG. 3, GREEN THREAD). String 1A, 3B, and 1A; skip 3A of Round 1, then pass down through the next A and up through the following A (FIG. 3, BLUE THREAD). String 1A, 1B, and 1A, then skip 1A of Round 1, pass down through the next A and up through the following A; repeat. Weave through beads to exit from the first 1A/2B/1A added in this round (FIG. 3, RED THREAD).

ROUND 3: String 1C and pass through the next 1A/1B (inner hole)/1A of Round 2; repeat. String 1C; pass through the next 1A/3B (inner holes)/1A of Round 2. String 1C and pass through the next 1A/1B (inner hole)/1A of Round 2; repeat. String 1C; pass through the next 1A/2B (inner holes) of Round 2, then step up through the outer hole of the second B (FIG. 4). *NOTE: The thread will now begin moving counterclockwise.*

ROUND 4: String 1B; pass through the outer hole of the next B of Round 2. String 2A, 1E, and 2A; pass through the outer hole of the following B of Round 2. String 1A, 1E, and 1A; pass through the outer hole of the next B of Round 2. String 2A, 1E, and 2A; pass through the outer hole of the following B of Round 2. String 1B and pass through the outer hole of the next B of Round 2; repeat. String 2A, 1E, and 2A; pass through the outer hole of the next B of Round 2. String 1A, 1E, and 1A; pass through the outer hole of the following B of Round 2. String 2A, 1E, and 2A; pass through the outer hole of the next B of Round 2. Weave through beads to exit from the B of Round 2 that sits right before the second B added in this round (FIG. 5, BLUE THREAD).

BOTTOM POINT: String 3A; pass through the outer hole of the second B added in Round 4. String 1B; pass through the outer hole of the next B added in Round 4. String 3A; pass through the outer hole of the nearest B of Round 2. Weave through beads to exit from the outer hole of the first B added in Round 4 (opposite the point just formed) (FIG. 5, RED THREAD).

LOOP: String 3A, 1D, 5A, and an ear wire; pass back through the D and the following A to form a loop. String 2A; pass through the last B exited (FIG. 6). Repeat the thread path to reinforce. Secure the thread and trim it.

❷ Repeat Step 1 for a second earring.

FIG. 1: Forming the thread base

FIG. 2: Stitching Round 1

FIG. 3: Adding Round 2

Artist's Tips

- You may substitute any of the 3mm, 4mm, 6mm, or 12mm beads with fire-polished rounds, crystal bicones, or pearl rounds.

- For a dramatic look, use bold jewel-tone colors.

FIG. 4: Forming Round 3

FIG. 5: Stitching Round 4 and the bottom point

FIG. 6: Adding the ear-wire loop and the ear wire

Crystal Cage

Lucy Joan King

technique
Right-angle weave

materials
2 g gold size 11° seed beads (A)

50 olivine 4mm crystal bicones (B)

16 Montana blue 4mm crystal bicones (C)

2 bright gold 10mm glass pearls

2 gold 10×15mm lever-back ear wires

Crystal 6 lb braided beading thread

tools
Scissors

Size 12 beading needle

FINISHED SIZE: 1½" (3.8cm)

① Sides

Right-angle-weave 2 bicone diamonds connected with seed beads:

DIAMOND 1, UNIT 1: Use 10' (3m) of thread to string 2B, 1C, and 1B, leaving a 6" (15cm) tail. Use the working and tail threads to tie a square knot, forming a tight circle. Weave through beads to exit from the C (FIG. 1, ORANGE THREAD).

DIAMOND 1, UNIT 2: String 3C; pass through the last C exited from the previous unit and the first 2C just added (FIG. 1, PURPLE THREAD).

DIAMOND 1, UNIT 3: String 3B; pass through the last C exited and the third C added in Unit 2 (FIG. 1, GREEN THREAD).

DIAMOND 1, UNIT 4: String 3B; pass through the last C exited and weave through beads to exit from the first C added in Unit 2 (FIG. 1, BLUE THREAD).

DIAMOND 1, UNIT 5: String 3B; pass through the last C exited and weave through beads to exit down through the outer B of Unit 3 (FIG. 1, RED THREAD).

LINK 1: String 3A, 1B, and 3A; pass through the last B exited and the first 3A and B just added (FIG. 2).

DIAMOND 2: Repeat Diamond 1, Units 1–5, this time using the B added in Link 1 as the first B of Unit 1.

② Cage

Use seed beads to link the diamonds' corners together, encasing a pearl:

LINK 2: String 3A; pass up through the first B of Diamond 1, Unit 1. String 3A; pass down through the last B exited on Diamond 2 (FIG. 3, BLUE THREAD). Repeat the thread path to reinforce. Weave through beads to exit from the corner B of Diamond 2, Unit 4 (FIG. 3, RED THREAD).

LINK 3: Repeat Link 2, connecting the corner B of Diamond 2, Unit 4, to the corner B of Diamond 1, Unit 4, and, before tightening, place 1 pearl in the center of the diamonds. Weave through beads to exit from the corner B of Diamond 2, Unit 5.

LINK 4: Repeat Link 2, connecting the corner B of Diamond 2, Unit 5, to the corner B of Diamond 1, Unit 5. Weave through beads to exit from the first 2A just added.

③ Loop

String 1A, 1B, 3A, an ear wire, and 3A; pass back through the B just added. String 1A; pass through the center A of the 3A strand opposite the one last exited. Pass back through the last A added (FIG. 4, BLUE THREAD). String 4A; pass back through the 3A/ear wire/3A. String 4A; pass back through the first A added in this step. Pass through the first A exited in this step (FIG. 4, RED THREAD). Repeat the thread path to reinforce. Secure the thread and trim.

④ Repeat Steps 1–3 for a second earring.

FIG. 1: Forming the first diamond

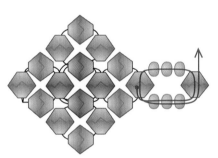

FIG. 2: Stitching Link 1

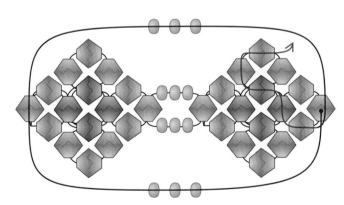

FIG. 3: Forming Link 2

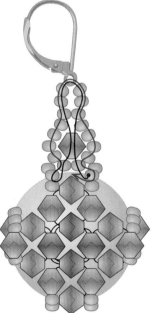

FIG. 4: Adding the ear-wire loop

MAIN COLORWAY

Swing Time

Christina Neit

techniques

Right-angle weave

Fringe

Picot

materials

1 g gold Duracoat size 15° seed beads (A)

2 g silver-lined rainbow golden bronze size 11° seed beads (B)

1 g gold metallic permanent-finish size 8° seed beads (C)

24 dark red coral 4mm crystal bicones (D)

6 gold-plated 4mm jump rings

2 gold-plated ¾" (2cm) ear wires

3¼" (8.5cm) of gold-plated 1.5×2.5mm curb chain

Smoke 6 lb braided beading thread

tools

Scissors

Size 11 and 12 beading needles

2 pairs of chain- or flat-nose pliers

Wire cutters

FINISHED SIZE: 2¾" (7cm)

① Swing

Work right-angle weave to form the earring dangle:

ROW 1: Use 5' (1.5m) of thread and B to form a strip of right-angle weave 8 units long. Exit up through the side B at the end of the strip.

ROW 2, FIRST PASS: String 3B; pass through the top B of the final unit in Row 1 (FIG. 1, BLUE THREAD). *String 1A; pass through the bottom B of the same Row 1 unit, back through the A just added, and through the top B of the same Row 1 unit. String 1A; pass through the top B of the following Row 1 unit. Repeat from * seven times, omitting the final A (FIG. 1, RED THREAD).

ROW 2, SECOND PASS: Flip the work horizontally so the beads added in this pass are on the reverse side of the beadwork. String 3B; pass down through the side B at the end of Row 1, Unit 1, and the bottom B of the same unit (FIG. 2, GREEN THREAD). String 1A; pass back through the top B of the same Row 1 unit and the A just added. Pass through the bottom B of the first Row 1 unit, back through the A just added, and back through the top B of the first Row 1 unit. Pass through the nearest A of Row 2's first pass and the top B of the next unit (FIG. 2, BLUE THREAD). String 1A, pass through the bottom B of the same Row 1 unit, back through the A just added, through the last top B exited, through the nearest A, and the top B of the following unit; repeat six times to add a second layer of A down the center of Row 1. *NOTE: This pass allows the earring to be reversible.* Weave through beads to exit from the bottom B of Row 1, Unit 8 (FIG. 2, RED THREAD).

ROW 3: String 2B, 1D, and 1B; pass back through the 1D and second B just added. String 1B; pass through the next bottom B of Row 1; repeat six times (FIG. 3, BLUE THREAD). Weave through beads, looping around threads as necessary to turn around, to exit from the bottom B of the final fringe formed in this row, toward the work (FIG. 3, RED THREAD).

ROW 4: String 1B, 1C, and 3B; pass through the C just added to form a picot. String 1B; pass through the bottom B of the next fringe in Row 3. Repeat from the beginning of this row five times. Weave through beads to exit from the bottom B of the final picot, toward the center (FIG. 4).

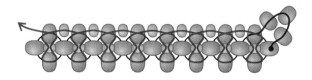

FIG. 1: Forming the first pass of Row 2

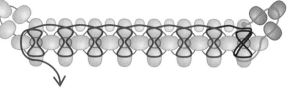

FIG. 2: Stitching the second pass of Row 2

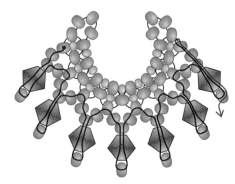

FIG. 3: Adding Row 3

FIG. 4: Forming Row 4

FIG. 5: Stitching the first pass of Row 5

FIG. 6: Adding the second pass of Row 5 and working Row 6

ROW 5, FIRST PASS: String 1A; pass through the C of the nearest picot, pass back through the A just added, and the B originally exited. String 1B, 1D, and 1B; pass through the bottom B of the next picot in Row 4. Repeat from the beginning of this row four times. String 1A; pass through the C of the nearest picot, pass back through the A just added, and the B originally exited (FIG. 5).

ROW 5, SECOND PASS: Flip the work horizontally so the beads added in this pass are on the reverse side of the beadwork. Repeat Row 5, first pass, this time only adding the A on the other side of the work and weaving through the sets of 1B/1D/1B. *NOTE: This pass, like the second pass in Row 2, makes the earring reversible.* Weave through beads to exit from the end 1B/1D/1B set, toward the center (FIG. 6, BLUE THREAD).

ROW 6: String 1B and pass through the next 1B/1D/1B set of Row 5; repeat three times (FIG. 6, RED THREAD). Secure the thread and trim.

2 Chain

Use 1 jump ring to connect one ¾" (2cm) piece of chain to the loop at the upper-left corner of the swing; repeat to connect a chain to the upper-right loop of the swing. Taking care that the chains aren't twisted, use 1 jump ring to connect the open ends of both chains to an ear wire.

3 Repeat Steps 1 and 2 for a second earring.

Artist's Tips

- If you'd rather, substitute the 3B added at the ends of Row 2 with 1C. Then when it's time, you can use a jump ring to connect the chain directly to the C.

- Change the look of these earrings by replacing the crystal bicones with glass pearls or fire-polished rounds. The bottom row of bicones could be replaced with Rizos, daggers, or long drops.

- Substitute the chain with strips of right-angle weave embellished with size 15° seed beads.

Briolette Bauble

Robijo Burzynski

techniques

Circular herringbone stitch

Circular peyote stitch

materials

2 g champagne galvanized size 11° Japanese cylinder beads (A)

2 crystal copper 12×8mm crystal rondelles

1 pair of gold-plated 10×16mm lever-back ear wires

Smoke 6 lb FireLine braided beading thread

Beading thread wax

tools

Scissors

Size 12 beading needle

FINISHED SIZE: 1¾" (4.5cm)

MAIN COLORWAY

❶ Earring Top

Use circular herringbone and peyote stitches to form the top half of the earring:

ROUND 1: Use 2' (61cm) of waxed thread to string 4A, leaving a 4" (10 cm) tail. Use the working and tail threads to tie a knot, forming a tight circle; pass through the first A strung (FIG. 1, GREEN THREAD).

ROUND 2: String 2A and pass through the next A of Round 1; repeat three times. *NOTE: Step up for this and subsequent rounds by passing through the first bead added in the current round (FIG. 1, BLUE THREAD).*

ROUND 3: String 2A and pass through the next A of Round 2 to form a herringbone stitch, then string 1A and pass through the following A to form a peyote stitch; repeat three times (FIG. 1, RED THREAD).

ROUND 4: String 2A and pass through the next A of the previous round, then work 2 peyote stitches with 1A in each stitch; repeat three times (FIG. 2, BLUE THREAD).

ROUND 5: String 2A and pass through the next A of the previous round, then work 3 peyote stitches with 1A in each stitch; repeat three times (FIG. 2, RED THREAD). Secure and trim the tail thread; don't trim the working thread. *NOTE: Rotate the beadwork clockwise so the thread exits at the right. In "Top edge" below, you'll use peyote stitch to add the 11A that will form the top edge of the top layer and then bend the beadwork; in "Zip" (again, below), you'll connect these beads with the opposite layer of Round 5 to form a smooth, rounded edge.*

TOP EDGE: String 1A and pass through the next A of Round 5; repeat ten times (FIG. 3). Bend the top half of the beadwork over the bottom half so you have 2 layers of beadwork. *NOTE: The first A just added will form the first corner of the earring top, the sixth A added will form the point, and the last A added forms the second corner.*

ZIP: Pinch the 2 layers of beadwork together so the beads of the top edge and the beads of the opposite layer of Round 5 interlock like a zipper. Weave through beads to form a seamless tube (FIG. 4; beads of Top Edge illustrated with an outline, and all other beads of the top layer removed for clarity). Weave through beads to exit from the sixth (point) A of the top edge. Rotate the beadwork so the thread exits at the top.

EAR WIRE: String 1A, an ear wire, and 1A and pass through the last A exited (FIG. 5); repeat the thread path multiple times to reinforce. Secure the thread and trim. Set aside.

FIG. 1: Stitching Rounds 1–3 of the earring top

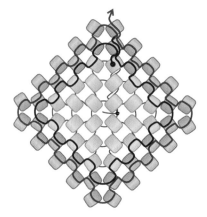

FIG. 2: Working Rounds 4 and 5 of the earring top

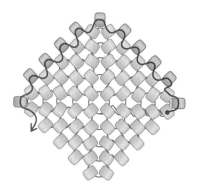

FIG. 3: Forming the top edge of the earring top

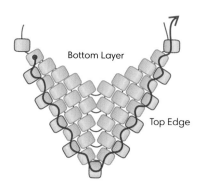

Bottom Layer

Top Edge

FIG. 4: Zipping the earring top

② Earring Bottom

Use circular herringbone and peyote stitches to form the bottom half of the earring:

ROUNDS 1–5: Repeat Earring Top, Rounds 1–5. Bend the top half of the beadwork over the bottom half so you have 2 layers of beadwork.

ROUND 6: String 1 A and pass through the next A of Round 5; repeat four times. String 1 corner A of the earring top and pass through the next A of Round 5 on the earring bottom. Work 4 peyote stitches with 1 A in each stitch. Repeat from the beginning of this round, working around the earring bottom from the top layer to the bottom layer and then the bottom layer to the top layer, and stringing the other corner A of the earring top. Pass through the first A of this round (FIG. 6; bottom layer removed for clarity).

RONDELLE: String 1 rondelle; pass through the mirror A of Round 6 on the earring bottom. Pass back through the rondelle and through the last A exited. Repeat this thread path multiple times to reinforce. Secure the thread and trim.

③ Repeat Steps 1 and 2 for a second earring.

variations

Try substituting a crystal disc for the rondelle.

For daintier earrings made of smaller components, stitch fewer rounds in the earring tops and bottoms and use 8mm rondelles.

To make a matching pendant, stitch one large earring bottom, stringing 1 A at each corner (instead of 1 corner A of the earring top) in Round 6. String a chain through the opening between the earring bottom and the rondelle.

FIG. 5: Adding the ear wire to the earring top

FIG. 6: Working Round 6 of the earring bottom

Peyote Star

Barbara Richard

techniques

Circular peyote stitch

Wireworking

materials

1 g dark bronze size 11° Japanese seed beads (A)

1 g gold size 11° Japanese seed beads (B)

2 vermeil 2×3mm cornerless rectangles

4 gold-filled 3.5mm jump rings

2 gold-filled 22-gauge 1½" head pins

1 pair of gold-filled ¾" (2cm) ear wires

Brown nylon beading thread

Beading wax

tools

Scissors

Size 12 beading needle

2 pairs of chain- or flat-nose pliers

Round-nose pliers

FINISHED SIZE: 2¼" (5.5cm)

① Large Star

Use circular peyote stitch to create a five-pointed star:

ROUND 1: Use 18" (45.5cm) of waxed thread to string 5A, leaving a 3" (7.5cm) tail. Tie a knot to form a tight circle. Pass through the first bead strung.

ROUND 2: String 1A and pass through the next A of Round 1; repeat four times for a total of 5A. Step up for the next and subsequent rounds by passing through the first bead added in the current round (FIG. 1, BLUE THREAD).

ROUND 3: Work 5 stitches with 2A in each stitch (FIG. 1, RED THREAD).

ROUND 4: Work 10 stitches with 1B in each stitch, splitting the pairs added in Round 3 (FIG. 2, GREEN THREAD).

ROUND 5: Work 1 stitch with 2B and 1 stitch with 1A; repeat four times for a total of 10B and 5A (FIG. 2, BLUE THREAD).

ROUND 6: String 1B, pass through the next B of Round 5, and weave through beads to exit between the next 2B pair; repeat four times for a total of 5B (FIG. 2, RED THREAD).Secure the thread and trim.

② Small Star

Use circular peyote stitch to form a smaller version of the large star:

ROUNDS 1-3: Using 18" (45.5cm) of waxed thread, repeat Step 1, Rounds 1–3.

ROUND 4: String 1B and pass through the next A of Round 3, A of Round 2, and A of Round 3; repeat four times for a total of 5B. Secure the thread and trim (FIG. 3).

③ Assembly

Attach 1 jump ring to the B at the tip of 1 point of the large star. Use 1 jump ring to connect the A opposite the previous jump ring on the large star to any B of Round 4 on the small star. *NOTE: If you have difficulty inserting the jump ring through the beads, pass a larger needle through the bead to compress the thread inside it.*

Use 1 head pin to string 1 rectangle; form a wrapped loop that attaches to the A directly below the previous jump ring. Attach an ear wire to the top jump ring (FIG. 4).

④ Repeat Steps 1–3 for a second earring.

FIG. 1: Working Rounds 1–3

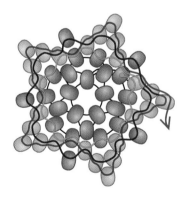

FIG. 2: Completing the large star

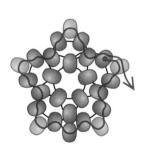

FIG. 3: Stitching the small star

variations

Create a necklace or bracelet with stones using the stars as spacers (shown in the amber and gold piece).

Brighten up your design by pairing silver-lined blue and red seed beads with metallic white Czech seed beads and silver findings.

FIG. 4: Assembling the earring

MAIN COLORWAY

Kumi Hoops

Sonia Corbin-Davis

techniques

Kumihimo braiding

Wireworking

materials

1 g matte blue iris size 11° seed beads (A)

2.5 g matte blue iris size 8° seed beads (B)

32 matte blue iris 4×7mm long magatama drops (C)

32 antiqued gold-plated 4×1mm daisy spacers (D)

2 antiqued gold-plated 10×8mm rectangular 2-sided fancy bead caps

2 brass 22-gauge 2" (5cm) head pins

1 pair of brass 22×20mm ear wires

Blue #18 twisted nylon bead cord

Smoke 6 lb braided beading thread

Multipurpose adhesive

tools

Scissors

Kumihimo braiding disc

3 oz weight

8 bead stops

8 kumihimo bobbins

Size 10 beading needle

Chain- or flat-nose pliers

Round-nose pliers

Wire cutters

FINISHED SIZE: 2⅜" (6cm)

STRINGING: Use 1 strand to *string 3A, 4B, 1D, 2C, 1D, 4B, and 3A, then place a bead stop on the strand. Using the same strand, string 3A, 4B, 1D, 2C, 1D, 4B, and 3A, then use the end of the cord to form a double-overhand knot and wrap it onto a bobbin. Repeat from * seven times using the other strands. Distribute the 8 strands as shown in the box on page 135 (FIG. A).

② Braiding

To start, follow the kumihimo braiding pattern shown in FIGS. B and C (see box on page 135) for ¼" (6mm) without adding beads. For the ninth and subsequent repeats, bring the top bead on each strand to the hole in the center of the disc. Slide the bead under the nearest strand that is crossed to the right or left; this locks each bead into place. After each turn, check the tension and bead position on the braid. Continue braiding until you reach the bead stops. Remove the bead stops and braid for ½" (1.3cm) without adding beads. *NOTE: This completes the braiding for 1 earring. Continue braiding with the beads as before.*

Remove the work from the disc and tie a double-overhand knot at the end of the kumihimo. Remove the bobbins. Dab the braided section without beads and the knots with adhesive; let dry. Cut the center of the braided section without beads to separate the work for 2 earrings. Trim the cord ends.

③ Assembly

Connect the braided ends and finish the earrings:

CONNECT: Add a needle to one end of 2' (61cm) of thread and tie a double-overhand knot on the other end of the thread. Pass through one end of 1 kumihimo braid near the knot, then pass through the other end of the braid near the knot to form a kumihimo loop. Continue to sew the braided ends together to secure (FIG. 1); secure the thread ends and trim. Center the sewn braid ends on a new 12" (30.5cm) piece of cord; use both cord ends to tie several square knots around the sewn braid; trim the tails.

EAR WIRES: Push 1 head pin up through the sewn braid of the kumihimo loop, from the center to the outside of the loop. String 1 bead cap; form a wrapped loop that attaches to an ear wire (FIG. 2).

Repeat this entire step using the remaining kumihimo braid for a second earring.

① Preparation

String the beads and prepare for braiding:

STRANDS: Cut four 48" (1.2m) strands of cord. Fold the cords in half and, holding the disc with the numbered side up, insert the folded center of the cords down through the disc's center hole. Hook the weight onto the folded center of the cords underneath the disc. *NOTE: The braid will form at the center hole, extending below the disc as you work. There will now be 8 strands.*

variations

Use flat peyote stitch to make bails that cover the knots of the kumihimo loops. Then stitch small seed bead loops that connect to the ear wires (shown, near right).

Use metal 10×5mm tubular bails in place of the bead caps (shown, top left). To do so, just omit the 12" (30.5cm) of cord that covers the knots at the end of Step 3, then dab the ends of the kumihimo braid with glue and insert them into each end of the bail; let dry.

FIG. 1: Connecting the braid ends

FIG. 2: Attaching the ear wire

Kumihimo Braiding 101

① Hold the disc parallel to the floor with number 32 held away from you. Tuck the strands into the slots around the disc and place the wire through the center hole (FIG. A). Adding a weight to the wire below the disc helps keep the correct tension. The braid will form at the center hole, extending below the disc as you work. Do not allow the strands to tangle, and keep the weight suspended.

② Move the bottom left strand between notches 16 and 17 up to the notch between 30 and 31. Move the top right strand between notches 32 and 1 down to the notch between 14 and 15 (FIG. B). Rotate the disc one-quarter turn clockwise so number 24 is now at the farthest (top) position, where number 32 used to be (shown at the top of FIG. C).

③ Move the bottom left strand between notches 8 and 9 up to the notch between 22 and 23. Move the top right strand between notches 24 and 25 down to the notch between 6 and 7 (FIG. C). Rotate the disc one-quarter turn clockwise.

④ Using the strands that are now the farthest and closest to you after the turn, repeat Steps 2 and 3 until the braid is the desired length.

⑤ When making beaded braids, slide each bead to the center hole and tuck it firmly under the strand that crosses to the right or left to lock the bead in place. Do not allow the bead to pop up.

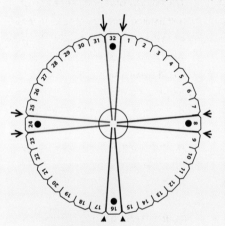

FIG. A: Load 1 strand into each of these slots: 7/8, 8/9, 15/16, 16/17 (blue thread), 23/24, 24/25, 31/32, and 32/1 (red thread).

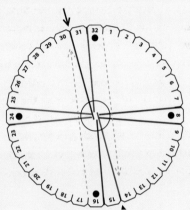

FIG. B: Moving the first two strands. The dotted green line shows the strand's movement from its starting point to its new position. New positions also marked by black arrows.

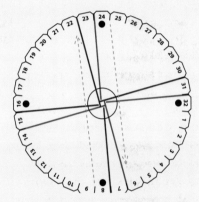

FIG. C: Moving the second two strands after making the quarter turn. The dotted green line shows the strand's movement from its starting point to its new position. After the next quarter turn, number 15 will be at the farthest (top) position.

Artist's Tips

- When gluing the knots, be careful not to get adhesive on the part of the braided cords directly next to the beads; you'll sew through this area to connect the ends of the braid.

- Substitute magatamas with lentils, Japanese drops, or size 6° seed beads for a different look.

- For larger earrings, add two beads to each section of A and B, but keep the same number of spacers as the original pattern.

- Choose a style of bead cap that will come down over the top edge of the loop and cover the knots.

MAIN COLORWAY

Incanto

Monica Vinci

techniques

Circular netting

Picot

Fringe

materials

3 g silver size 15° seed beads (A)

18 silver size 11° seed beads (B)

1 g lilac Picasso 5×2.5mm 2-hole seed beads (C)

12 cyclamen opal 3mm crystal bicones (D)

2 foil-back amethyst 12mm crystal rivolis

28 powder rose 4mm crystal pearl rounds (E)

24 blackberry 4mm crystal pearl rounds (F)

8 white 6mm crystal pearl rounds (G)

16 chalk white pink luster 8×4mm piggy beads (H)

2 amethyst gold luster 6mm 3-cut faceted pressed-glass rounds

1 pair of silver-plated 4mm crystal rhinestone ear posts

Rose size B nylon beading thread

tools

Size 12 beading needle

Scissors

FINISHED SIZE: 1 ¼ × 2½"
(3.2 × 6.5cm)

❶ Body

Use circular netting to bezel a rivoli for the earring body:

BODY ROUND 1: Use 3' (91.5cm) of thread to string {1G and 1B} four times, leaving a 4" (10cm) tail. Use the working and tail threads to tie a knot, forming a tight circle. Pass through the first G strung (FIG. 1).

BODY ROUND 2: String 1A, 1F, 1A, 1E, 1A, 1F, and 1A; pass through the last G exited and the following 1B/1G of Body Round 1. Repeat from the beginning of this round three times. Step up by passing through the first 1A/1F/1A/1E/1A/1F (FIG. 2, GREEN THREAD).

BODY ROUND 3: String 2H (side hole inside to outside, then side hole outside to inside) and pass through the next 1F/1A/1E/1A/1F of Body Round 2; repeat three times. *NOTE: Each H has a hole through the center of the bead and a hole through one side of the bead. We'll refer to them as the center hole and the side hole, respectively. For this round, you'll pass through only the side hole of each H.* Weave through beads to exit from the next E of Body Round 2 (FIG. 2, BLUE THREAD).

BODY ROUND 4: String 1A, 1F, and 1A, then pass through the next E of Body Round 2; repeat three times (FIG. 2, RED THREAD). Place 1 rivoli faceup into the beadwork so the face touches this round. Snug the beads so this round tightens around the rivoli. Repeat the thread path of this round to reinforce. Weave through beads to exit from the center hole of the first H in the 2H pair at the top of the beadwork, toward the next H in the pair.

❷ Embellishment

Use circular netting, picot, and fringe to embellish the earring body:

EMBELLISHMENT ROUND 1, STITCH 1: String 1A, 2C, and 1A; pass through the center hole of the next H in Body Round 3 (FIG. 3, YELLOW THREAD).

EMBELLISHMENT ROUND 1, STITCH 2: String 1E, 1D, and 3A; pass through the D just strung. String 1E; pass through the center hole of the next H in Body Round 3 (FIG. 3, BROWN THREAD).

EMBELLISHMENT ROUND 1, STITCHES 3 AND 4: String 1A, 1C, and 1A; pass through the center hole of the next H in Body Round 3. Repeat Embellishment Round 1, Stitch 2 (FIG. 3, ORANGE THREAD).

EMBELLISHMENT ROUND 1, STITCHES 5-8: Repeat Embellishment Round 1, Stitches 1-4. Step up through the first A of Embellishment Round 1 (FIG. 3, PURPLE THREAD).

EMBELLISHMENT ROUND 2, STITCH 1: String 3A; pass through the second (outside) hole of the nearest C in the previous round. String 1C; pass through the outside hole of the next C in the previous round. String 3A; pass through the next A of the previous round and the center hole of the nearest H. Weave through beads to exit from the first A of Embellishment Round 1, Stitch 3 (FIG. 3, GREEN THREAD).

EMBELLISHMENT ROUND 2, STITCH 2: String 3A; pass through the outside hole of the nearest C. String 3A; pass through the next 1A/1H (center hole) of the previous rounds. Weave through beads to exit from the next H (center hole) and 1A (FIG. 3, BLUE THREAD).

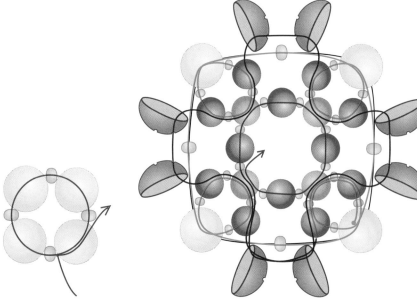

FIG. 1: Forming body Round 1

FIG. 2: Working body Rounds 2–4

FRINGE DROP: String 3A; pass through the outside hole of the nearest C in Embellishment Round 1. String 1A, 1B, 1E, 1D, 1 pressed-glass round, 1D, 1E, and 1A; skip 1A and pass back through the 1E/1D/pressed-glass round/1D/1E/1B just strung. String 1A; pass through the outside hole of the next C in Embellishment Round 1. String 3A; pass through the next 1A/1H (center hole) of the previous rounds. Weave through beads to exit from the next H (center hole) and 1A.

EMBELLISHMENT ROUND 2, STITCH 3: Repeat Embellishment Round 2, Stitch 2. Pass through the first 3A of Embellishment Round 2, Stitch 1 (FIG. 3, RED THREAD).

BAIL: String 4A: pass through the outside hole of the C in Embellishment Round 2, Stitch 1. String 4A; pass through the next 3A of Embellishment Round 2, Stitch 1. Weave through beads to exit from the first 4A of this stitch (FIG. 4, BLUE THREAD). String 2B, an ear post, and 2B; pass through the last 4A added and weave through beads to exit from the first 4A of this stitch. Pass through the nearest 2B/ear post/1B just added, skip 1B, then pass through the outside hole of the nearest C. Skip the first B added and pass through the following 1B/ear post/1B again (FIG. 4, RED THREAD). Repeat the thread path to reinforce. Secure the thread and trim.

3 Repeat Steps 1 and 2 for a second earring.

FIG. 3: Adding embellishment Rounds 1 and 2 and the fringe drop

FIG. 4: Forming the bail

Swinging Chevron

Sue A. Neel

techniques
Tubular peyote stitch

Wireworking

materials
4 g light metallic bronze size 11°
Japanese cylinder beads (A)

4 g turquoise size 11° Japanese cylinder
beads (B)

4 copper 22-gauge 1½" (cm) head pins

8 copper 22-gauge 1½" (cm) eye pins

2 copper 5mm unsoldered jump rings

2" (5cm) of copper 2×3mm oval chain

1 pair of copper 17mm ear wires

Crystal 6 lb FireLine braided beading
thread

tools
Scissors

Size 12 beading needle

2 pairs of chain- or flat-nose
pliers

Round-nose pliers

Wire cutters

FINISHED SIZE: 3" (7.5cm)

① Bottom Tier

Use tubular peyote stitch to form the largest, bottom tier of the earring:

ROUND 1: Use 5' (cm) of thread to string {4A and 4B} twice, leaving an 8" (cm) tail. Pass through the beads again and use the working and tail threads to tie a loose knot. Pass through the first 2A strung (FIG. 1, GREEN THREAD). *Note: In Rounds 2–13, increases will occur on the right edge of the beadwork, and decreases will occur on the left edge.*

ROUND 2: String 2A; pass through the next A of the previous round. *Note: This will become the increasing edge.* Work 2 peyote stitches with 1B in each stitch and 1 stitch with 1A. Skip the next 2A of the previous round; pass through the following A. *Note: This will become the decreasing edge.* Work 1 stitch with 1A and 2 stitches with 1B in each stitch. Pass through the first A of this round (FIG. 1, BLUE THREAD). *Note: When working the following rounds, pinch the long (turquoise) sides of the beadwork together to form a tight double-layered strip.*

ROUND 3: String 2A; pass through the next A of the previous round. Work 2 stitches with 1B in each stitch and 1 stitch with 1A. Pass through the next A of the previous round. Work 1 stitch with 1A and 2 stitches with 1B in each stitch. Pass through the first A of this round (FIG. 1, RED THREAD).

ROUNDS 4–13: Repeat Round 3 ten times for a total of 13 rounds. Pass through the second A added in Round 13. *Note: The first 2A added in Round 13 form the bottom point of the tier. In the following rounds, the increasing and decreasing edges will be opposite than in the previous rounds; this forms the "V" shape.*

ROUND 14: *Note: In Rounds 14–25, increases will occur on the left edge of the beadwork, and decreases will occur on the right edge.* Work 1 stitch with 1A and 2 stitches with 1B in each stitch. String 2A; pass through the next A of the previous round. *Note: This will become the increasing edge.* Work 2 stitches with 1B in each stitch and 1 stitch with 1A. Pass through the next A of the previous round and the first A added in this round (FIG. 2, BLUE THREAD); Rounds 1–12 removed for clarity).

ROUND 15: Work 1 stitch with 1A and 2 stitches with 1B in each stitch. String 2A; pass through the next A of the previous round. Work 2 stitches with 1B in each stitch and 1 stitch with 1A. Pass through the next A of the previous round and the first A of this round (FIG. 2, RED THREAD).

ROUNDS 16-25: Repeat Round 15 ten times.

END 1: *Note: You'll notice that you've formed a double-layered piece of beadwork; at this stage, the ends look unfinished. To form a smooth, rounded end, you'll use peyote stitch to add 3 beads to 1 layer of Round 25, then zip these 3 end beads to the opposite layer of Round 25; these 3 beads will also be used as a connection point for the tiers.* Work 1 stitch with 1A and 2 stitches with 1B in each stitch. Pass through the next A of Round 25 (FIG. 3, BLUE THREAD; for clarity, Rounds 1–24 are not included).

END ZIP 1: Pinch the 2 layers of this end of the beadwork together so that the beads of End 1 and the beads of the opposite layer in Round 25 interlock like a zipper. Weave through the beads to form a seamless edge (FIG. 3, RED THREAD). Secure the working thread and trim. *Note: When tying off your threads, avoid passing through beads of End 1 again; you'll want the holes to be as clear as possible when using these beads to connect the tiers in Step 4.*

END 2: Use the tail thread to repeat End 1, working off of Round 1.

END ZIP 2: Repeat End Zip 1 to zip the beads of End 2 and the opposite layer of Round 1.

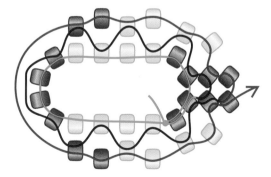

FIG. 1: Working Rounds 1–3 of the bottom tier

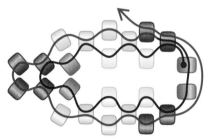

FIG. 2: Forming Rounds 14 and 15 of the bottom tier

FIG. 3: Stitching End 1 and zipping the end

2 Middle Tier

Repeat Bottom Tier, Rounds 1–11. Repeat Bottom Tier, Rounds 14–23. Repeat End 1, End Zip 1, End 2, and End Zip 2 of the bottom tier.

3 Top Tier

Use 4' (cm) of thread to repeat Bottom Tier, Rounds 1–9. Repeat Bottom Tier, Rounds 14–21. Repeat End 1, End Zip 1, End 2, and End Zip 2 of the bottom tier.

4 Assembly

Use head pins and eye pins to connect the tiers at each end via the beads added in End 1 and End 2:

CONNECTION 1: Holding the bottom tier in your nondominant hand with the "V" pointing down, use 1 head pin to pass up through the 1A/1B/1B of End 1. Use pliers to form a simple loop on the head pin, after the last B exited (FIG. 4, PURPLE HEAD PIN; side view of tiers shown and all other beads removed for clarity).

CONNECTION 2: Holding the middle tier in your nondominant hand with the "V" pointing down, use 1 eye pin to pass up through the 1A/1B/1B of End 1. Form a simple loop on the eye pin, after the last B exited. Attach the eye of the eye pin to the simple loop formed in Connection 1 (FIG. 4, GREEN EYE PIN).

CONNECTION 3: Repeat Connection 2, using the top tier and attaching it to the middle tier (FIG. 4, RED EYE PIN).

Repeat this entire step to connect End 2 of each tier.

5 Finish

Separate the chain into two 3-link pieces. Attach 1 piece of chain to 1 simple loop formed in Connection 3, above the top tier; repeat using the second piece of chain and the second simple loop. Use 1 jump ring to connect the other end of each piece of chain to 1 ear wire (FIG. 5).

6 Repeat Steps 1–5 for a second earring.

variation

To make a matching pendant, omit Step 5 and instead attach one end of a long piece of chain to one simple loop formed in Connection 3, above the top tier. Attach the other end of the chain to the other simple loop above the top tier.

FIG. 4: Assembling the tiers

FIG. 5: Finishing the earring

Waxing Crescent Moon

Penny Dixon

techniques

Cubic right-angle weave

Circular peyote stitch

Fringe

Netting

materials

1 g bronze size 15° Japanese seed beads (A)

2 g green luster opaque hybrid size 11° Japanese seed beads (B)

1 g bronze size 11° Japanese seed beads (C)

2 g bronze size 8° Japanese seed beads (D)

22 matte metallic bronze iris 10×3mm 2-hole crescent beads (E)

20 milky rose bronze vega 3mm fire-polished rounds (F)

2 amethyst gold suede 6mm pressed-glass rounds (G)

1 pair of vintage brass 11×20mm ear wires

Smoke 6 lb FireLine braided beading thread

tools

Scissors

Size 11 beading needle

2 pairs of chain- or flat-nose pliers

FINISHED SIZE: 2½" (6.5cm)

MAIN COLORWAY

① Teardrop

Use cubic right-angle weave and circular peyote stitch to form the top of the earring:

CUBE 1, BOTTOM: Use 4' (1.2m) of thread to string 4B, leaving an 8" (20.5cm) tail; pass through the beads again to form a tight circle, then pass through the first B strung (FIG. 1, PURPLE THREAD).

CUBE 1, FACE 1: String 1C and 2B; pass through the last B exited and the next B at the bottom of this cube (FIG. 1, GREEN THREAD).

CUBE 1, FACE 2: String 2B; pass down through the C of the previous face and pass through the last B exited at the bottom of this cube and the next B (FIG. 1, BLUE THREAD).

CUBE 1, FACE 3: String 2B; pass down through the nearest B of the previous face and pass through the last B exited at the bottom of this cube and the next B. Pass up through the nearest B of the first face in this cube (FIG. 1, RED THREAD).

CUBE 1, FACE 4 AND TOP: String 1B; pass down through the nearest B of the previous face, pass through the last B exited at the bottom of this cube, pass up through the next B of the first face in this cube, and pass through the following B at the top of the first cube (FIG. 2, BLUE THREAD). Pass back through the 4B at the top of this cube, exiting from the top B of Face 1 (FIG. 2, RED THREAD). *NOTE: Make sure you're always exiting toward the corner C before starting the next cube.*

CUBE 2, FACE 1: *NOTE: The B at the top of the previous cube will act as the bottom of this cube. Repeat Cube 1, Face 1 (FIG. 3, GREEN THREAD).*

CUBE 2, FACE 2: Repeat Cube 1, Face 2 (FIG. 3, BLUE THREAD).

CUBE 2, FACE 3: Repeat Cube 1, Face 3 (FIG. 3, RED THREAD).

CUBE 2, FACE 4 AND TOP: Repeat Cube 1, Face 4 (FIG. 4, BLUE THREAD) and Top (FIG. 4, RED THREAD).

CUBES 3–10: Repeat Cube 2, Faces 1–4 and Top eight times. Bend the beadwork into a horseshoe shape so that the C of the cubes sit at the top, interior of the horseshoe with Cube 1 on the right and Cube 10 on the left. Pass through the nearest B of Cube 10, Top to exit toward the bottom outside edge of the horseshoe.

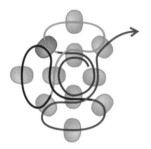

FIG. 1: Stitching Cube 1, Bottom and Faces 1–3 of the teardrop

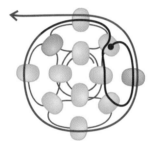

FIG. 2: Forming Cube 1, Face 4 and top of the teardrop

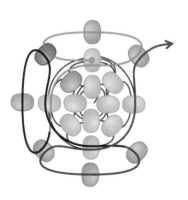

FIG. 3: Working Cube 2, Faces 1–3 of the teardrop

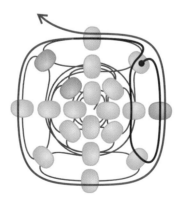

FIG. 4: Adding Cube 2, Face 4 and top of the teardrop

FIG. 5: Stitching the join top of the teardrop

JOIN TOP: String 2B and pass through the B of Cube 1, Bottom that mirrors the last B exited in Cube 10, Top, then pass through the last B exited in Cube 10; repeat the thread path to close the shape and pass through the first B just added (FIG. 5).

JOIN UNIT 1: String 2B; pass up through the nearest outside end B of Cube 10, the last B exited in Join Top, and the first B just added (FIG. 6, BLUE THREAD).

JOIN UNIT 2: String 1B; pass up through the nearest outside end B of Cube 1, pass back through the second B of Join Top, and pass down through the first B of Join Unit 1 (the bottom tip of the teardrop). Pass through the B of this unit to exit toward the back of the beadwork (FIG. 6, RED THREAD).

JOIN BOTTOM: Flip the beadwork facedown. Pass through the nearest 4B on the center back of the teardrop to close the bottom side of the join. Weave through beads to exit from the B of Cube 1, Bottom that's on the top edge of the teardrop, exiting toward the center (see FIG. 7 red start dot). Flip the beadwork faceup.

TEARDROP CENTER: String 1C; pass through the C of Cubes 1–10 and pass back through the last C added (FIG. 7). Pull the beads snug. Flip the beadwork facedown. Weave through beads to exit from a bottom-right B on the bottom join, toward the tip of the teardrop (see FIG. 8 green start dot).

OUTSIDE ROUND: String 1D and pass through the next B along the outside bottom edge; repeat eleven times. Pass through the first D added (FIG. 8, GREEN THREAD; back of beadwork shown).

② Ring

Use fringe and netting to form a ring-shaped component embellished with crescents:

FRINGE: String 2A, 1G, and 1A; skip the last A added and pass back through the G. String 2A; pass through the last D exited and the next 1B/1D (FIG. 8, BLUE THREAD).

ROUND 1: String 3A, 22D, and 3A; pass through the bottom-right D of the teardrop. Weave through beads to exit from the first D of this round (FIG. 8, RED THREAD). Flip the beadwork faceup.

Artist's Tips

- When beginning the teardrop, hold the tail thread tight until the first cube is finished. If you prefer to knot your starting thread, you may do so after stringing the first four beads.

- Tight tension is a must when working Step 2.

FIG. 6: Forming Join Units 1 and 2 of the teardrop

FIG. 7: Working the teardrop center

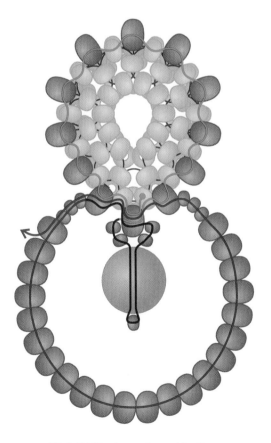

FIG. 8: Finishing the teardrop, adding the fringe, and beginning the ring

ROUND 2: *NOTE: You should be working clockwise for the crescents added in this round to be oriented correctly.* Lay 11E horizontally on your work surface with each bead's inside curve facing upward. String 1E (left hole) and 1A, then skip the A just added, pass back through the last (left) hole exited in the E just added, and pass through the next 2D of Round 1 (FIG. 9, BLUE THREAD); repeat ten times. *NOTE: At the end of the final repeat, you'll pass through the nearest 1D/3A in Round 1 instead of 2D.* Weave through beads to exit from the first A of this round (FIG. 9, RED THREAD).

ROUND 3: String 1F and pass through the next A of Round 2; repeat nine times. Pass through the nearest hole of the next E and weave through beads to exit up through the second-to-last D of Step 1, Outside Round (FIG. 10, GREEN THREAD).

ROUND 4: String 3A; pass through the second (outside) hole of the nearest E from front to back. String 6A and pass through the outside hole (front to back) of the next E; repeat nine times. String 3A; pass down through the third D of Step 1, Outside Round. Weave through beads to exit from the seventh D of Step 1, Outside Round at the top of the teardrop (FIG. 10, BLUE THREAD).

EAR-WIRE LOOP: String 7A; pass through the D just exited and repeat the thread path to reinforce the loop (FIG. 10, RED THREAD). Secure the threads and trim. Attach an ear wire to the loop just formed by opening and closing the loop of the ear wire as you would a jump ring.

3 Repeat Steps 1 and 2 for a second earring, but this time in Step 2, Round 2, string the E through the right hole first so the crescents will fan in the opposite direction and the earrings will mirror each other.

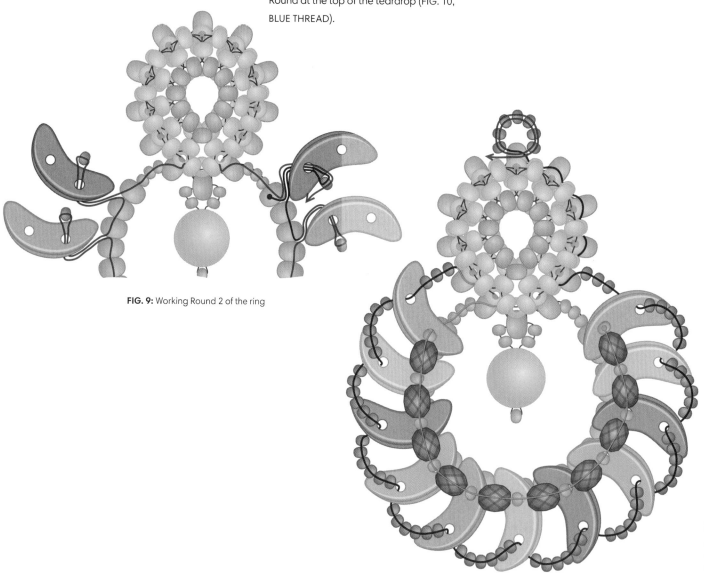

FIG. 9: Working Round 2 of the ring

FIG. 10: Forming Rounds 3 and 4 of the ring and stitching the ear-wire loop

Evening Star

Agnieszka Watts

techniques

Tubular netting

Fringe

materials

3 g metallic hematite size 15° Japanese seed beads (A)

1 g gold luster size 15° Japanese seed beads (B)

2 topaz 4mm crystal bicones

6 ruby AB 6mm crystal bicones

2 cyclamen opal 6mm crystal rounds

2 foil-back crystal volcano 18mm crystal rivolis

2 hematite 6×16mm pressed-glass daggers

1 pair of antiqued sterling silver 10×18mm decorative ear wires

Black size D nylon beading thread

tools

Scissors

Size 11 or 12 beading needles

FINISHED SIZE: 4" (10cm)

① Large Component

Use tubular netting to form a bezel around a rivoli:

ROUND 1: Use 3' (91.5cm) of thread to string 12A, leaving a 4" (10cm) tail. Pass through the beads again to form a tight circle; use the working and tail threads to tie a square knot and pass through the first A strung (FIG. 1).

ROUND 2: String 3A, skip 1A of the previous round, and pass through the following A; repeat five times for a total of 6 nets. Step up by passing through the first 2A added in this round (FIG. 2).

ROUND 3: String 5A and pass through the center (second) A of the nearest Round 2 net; repeat five times for a total of 6 nets. Step up through the first 3A added in this round (FIG. 3, GREEN THREAD).

ROUND 4: String 9A and pass through the center (third) A of the nearest Round 3 net; repeat five times for a total of 6 nets. Step up through the first 5A added in this round (FIG. 3, BLUE THREAD).

ROUND 5: String 9A and pass through the center (fifth) A of the nearest Round 4 net; repeat five times for a total of 6 nets. Step up through the first 5A added in this round (FIG. 3, RED THREAD).

ROUND 6: Place 1 rivoli faceup into the beadwork. Hold the rivoli in position with your thumb and forefinger and pull the thread tight to bezel the rivoli. String 7A and pass through the center (fifth) A of the nearest Round 5 net; repeat five times for a total of 6 nets. Step up through the first 4A added in this round (FIG. 4, BLUE THREAD).

ROUND 7: String 5A and pass through the center (fourth) A of the nearest Round 6 net; repeat five times for a total of 6 nets. Weave through beads to exit from the seventh A of a Round 5 net (FIG. 4, RED THREAD).

② Ear Wire

String 5A, an ear wire, and 5A; skip the last 2A of the current Round 5 net and the first 2A of the next Round 5 net, then pass through the nearest 7A of Round 5. Weave through beads and repeat the thread path to reinforce. Weave through beads to exit from the center A of the bottom-left Round 4 net (FIG. 5). Do not trim the thread. Set aside.

③ Small Component

Stitch seed beads and a crystal round to form the small component:

ROUNDS 1–3: Repeat Rounds 1–3 of the large component.

FIG. 1: Forming Round 1 of the large component

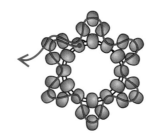

FIG. 2: Stitching Round 2 of the large component

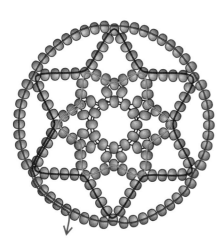

FIG. 3: Working Rounds 3–5 of the large component

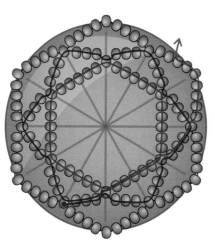

FIG. 4: Bezeling the front of the large component (Rounds 6 and 7)

FIG. 5: Adding the ear wire

ROUND 4: String 7A and pass through the center (third) A of the nearest Round 3 net; repeat five times for a total of 6 nets. Weave through beads to exit from 1A of Round 1 that sits beneath a Round 2 net (FIG. 6).

ROUNDS 5 AND 6: Repeat Rounds 2 and 3 using B to add a second layer to this component. Weave through beads to exit from 1A of Round 1 (FIG. 7, BLUE THREAD).

CENTER: String 1 crystal round; pass through the opposite 1A of Round 1, then pass back through the crystal round just added, and through the first 1A exited from Round 1. Repeat the thread path to reinforce. Weave through beads to exit from the third A of a Round 3 net (FIG. 7, RED THREAD).

④ Fringe Drop

String 4A, 1 ruby bicone, 2A, 1 topaz bicone, 4A, 1 dagger, and 3A; skip 3A and pass back through the first A of the last 4A, the topaz bicone, 2A, the ruby bicone, and the first 4A just added. Pass through the last A exited from Round 3 (FIG. 8). Weave through beads and repeat the thread path to reinforce. Secure the thread and trim.

⑤ Connect

Use the working thread from the small component to *string 2A, 1 ruby bicone, and 2A; pass through the center A in the top-left Round 4 net of the small component, back through the 2A/bicone/2A just added, and through the last A exited on the large component. Repeat the thread path to reinforce, then weave through beads of the large component to exit from the center A in the bottom-right Round 4 net (FIG. 9, BLUE THREAD). Repeat from * to connect the large component to the center A in the top-right Round 4 net of the small component (FIG. 9, RED THREAD). Secure the thread and trim.

⑥ Repeat Steps 1–5 for a second earring.

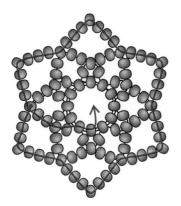

FIG. 6: Working Round 4 of the small component

FIG. 7: Stitching Rounds 5 and 6 and the center of the small component

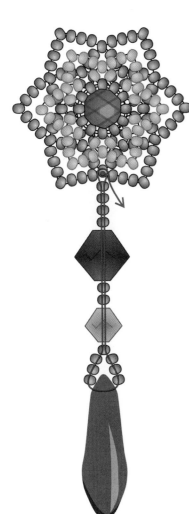

FIG. 8: Adding the fringe drop

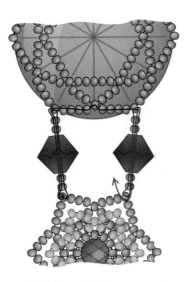

FIG. 9: Connecting the components

MAIN COLORWAY

Ancient Portals

Kassie Shaw

techniques

Tubular and circular netting

Picot

Right-angle weave

materials

1 g purple permanent-finish size 15° Japanese seed beads (A)

2 g silver-lined light gray size 11° Japanese seed beads (B)

2 g nickel size 11° Japanese seed beads (C)

14 metallic blue saturated 10×3mm 2-hole crescent beads (D)

2 foil-back tanzanite 12mm crystal rivolis

24 blue iris 2mm fire-polished rounds (E)

2 silver 22-gauge 4mm jump rings

2 silver 22×20mm ear wires

13" (33cm) of silver-plated 1.3mm curb chain

Purple One-G nylon beading thread

tools

Scissors

Size 12 sharp (short) beading needle

FINISHED SIZE: 3" (7.5cm)

① Earring

Use netting, picots, and right-angle weave to bezel and embellish a rivoli:

ROUND 1: Lay 7D horizontally on your work surface with each bead's inside curve facing down. Working counterclockwise, use 4' (1.2m) of thread to string 3B and 1D (right hole); repeat six times, leaving a 6" (15cm) tail. Use the working and tail threads to tie a knot and pass through the first 3B strung (FIG. 1, BLUE THREAD).

ROUND 2: String 2B; pass through the second (inside) hole of the nearest D. Skip the next 2B of the previous round and pass through the following B. Repeat from the beginning of this round six times. Pass through the first 2B of this round (FIG. 1, RED THREAD). Pull the thread snug to tighten the beadwork.

ROUND 3: String 2C and pass through the second B of the next 2B in the previous round; repeat six times (FIG. 2, BLUE THREAD). *NOTE: Take care that the thread and the C pass under the D of Round 1. Repeat the thread path of this round to reinforce, tightening the beads into a ring. Pass through the nearest D (inside hole) and pass down through the following 3B, exiting toward the back of the beadwork (FIG. 2, RED THREAD). Flip the beadwork over. Insert 1 rivoli facedown into the beadwork so the front of the rivoli touches Round 3.*

ROUND 4: String 2C and pass back through the first B of the next 3B in Round 1 to exit toward the center of the beadwork; repeat six times (FIG. 3; back of beadwork shown). *NOTE: Take care that the thread and the C pass under the D of Round 1.*

ROUND 5: String 9A and pass down through the nearest 5B of Rounds 1 and 2, then pass through the next 2C of Round 4 and pass back through the following B of Round 1 to exit toward the center of the beadwork (FIG. 4; back of beadwork shown); repeat six times. Pass through the first 5A of this round. *NOTE: You'll now begin working clockwise.*

ROUND 6: String 4B and pass through the fifth A of the next 9A set in the previous round; repeat six times. Pass through the first 4B of this round (FIG. 5, BLUE THREAD; back of beadwork shown).

ROUND 7: String 2C and pass through the next 4B of the previous round; repeat six times. Pass through the first C of this round (FIG. 5, RED THREAD). Flip the beadwork faceup. *NOTE: You'll now begin working counterclockwise.*

FIG. 1: Stitching Rounds 1 and 2

FIG. 2: Working Round 3

FIG. 3: Forming Round 4

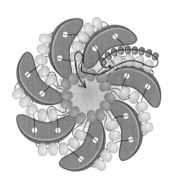

FIG. 4: Adding Round 5

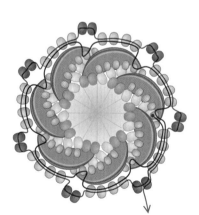

FIG. 5: Stitching Rounds 6 and 7

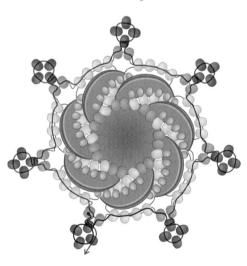

FIG. 6: Working Round 8

ROUND 8: String 4C; pass through the first C just added to form a picot, the nearest C of the previous round, the next 4B of Round 6, and the following C of the previous round (FIG. 6, BLUE THREAD). Repeat from the beginning of this round six times. Pass through the first 2C of this round (FIG. 6, RED THREAD).

ROUND 9: String 3C, then pass through the last C exited and the first 2C just added (FIG. 7, PURPLE THREAD); repeat (FIG. 7, GREEN THREAD). String 1C; pass through the nearest C of the next picot in Round 8. String 1C; pass through the last C exited, the first C just added, and the next 3C of the nearest picot (FIG. 7, BLUE THREAD). Repeat from the beginning of this round four times (FIG. 7, RED THREAD). *NOTE: You'll now begin working clockwise. Rotate the beadwork clockwise so the thread exits at the right.*

ROUND 10, PREPARE: Cut two 2" (5cm) pieces of chain and one 2½" (6.5cm) piece of chain. Set aside.

ROUND 10, SECTION 1: *NOTE: Always pass through the outside C of the nearest picot or right-angle-weave unit unless otherwise noted.* String 1A and pass through the nearest C, then string 1E and pass through the next C; repeat (FIG. 8, TURQUOISE THREAD). String 1A; pass through the nearest C (FIG. 8, PINK THREAD).

ROUND 10, SECTION 2: String 1E and one 2" (5cm) piece of chain; pass through the nearest C. String 1A; pass through the nearest C (FIG. 8, ORANGE THREAD).

ROUND 10, SECTION 3: Repeat Round 10, Section 2 using the 2½" (6.5cm) piece of chain (FIG. 8, PURPLE THREAD).

ROUND 10, SECTION 4: String 1E and the remaining 2" (5cm) piece of chain; pass through the nearest C. String 1E and pass through the nearest C; repeat (FIG. 8, GREEN THREAD).

ROUND 10, SECTION 5: String the last link of the first piece of chain in this round, taking care that the chain isn't twisted, and 1E; pass through the nearest C. String 1A; pass through the nearest C (FIG. 8, BLUE THREAD).

ROUND 10, SECTIONS 6 AND 7: Repeat Round 10, Section 5 twice, stringing each subsequent piece of chain (FIG. 8, RED THREAD).

ROUND 10, SECTION 8: String 1E and pass through the nearest C, then string 1A and pass through the next C; repeat. *NOTE: On the last repeat, you'll pass through the outside C of the picot (FIG. 8, YELLOW THREAD). Secure the threads and trim them.*

② Ear Wire

Use 1 jump ring to attach an ear wire to the center C of the picot in Round 8 that isn't connected to right-angle-weave units. *NOTE: Take care that the front of the ear wire faces the same direction as the front of the rivoli.*

③ Repeat Steps 1 and 2 for a second earring, but work clockwise in Round 1 and string the left hole of the D so the earrings swirl in the opposite direction. Work all subsequent rounds in the opposite direction as well.

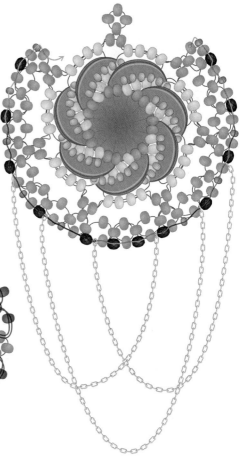

FIG. 7: Forming Round 9

FIG. 8: Adding Round 10

Flower Basket

Barbara Falkowitz

techniques

Circular peyote stitch

Wireworking

materials

1 g silver-lined matte brown size 11° seed beads (A)

5 g beige Picasso 5×2mm 2-hole seed beads (B)

5 g turquoise luster 5×2mm 2-hole seed beads (C)

4 crystal bronze shade 4mm crystal bicones (D)

2 opaque rose luster 5mm glass melon rounds

2 antiqued copper 6×1.5mm bead caps

2 antiqued copper 24-gauge 2" (5cm) head pins

8 antiqued copper 4mm jump rings

4 antiqued copper 6mm jump rings

5" (12.5cm) of gunmetal 24-gauge craft wire

9" (23cm) of antiqued copper 3×5mm etched oval chain

1 pair of antiqued copper ¾" (2cm) decorative lever-back ear wires

Smoke 6 lb braided beading thread

tools

Scissors

Size 10 beading needle

Round-nose pliers

2 pairs of chain- or flat-nose pliers

Wire cutters

FINISHED SIZE: 3½" (9cm)

❶ Front

Use circular peyote stitch to form the front of
a beaded bead:

ROUND 1: Use 20" (51cm) of thread to string
8B, leaving a 3" (7.5cm) tail; pass through
the beads again to form a tight circle and
use the working and tail threads to tie a
knot (FIG. 1, BLUE THREAD). Secure and
trim the tail thread.

CENTER: String 1D; pass through the inside
hole of the opposite B in Round 1. Step up
through the outside hole of the same B
(FIG. 1, RED THREAD).

ROUND 2: String 1C and pass through the
outside hole of the next B in Round 1;
repeat seven times for a total of 8C
(FIG. 2, BLUE THREAD).

ROUND 3: String 1A and pass through the
outside hole of the next B in Round 1;
repeat seven times for a total of 8A (FIG. 2,
RED THREAD). *NOTE: Make sure the A are
on the same side of the beadwork as the D.*
Secure the thread and trim. Set the front
of the earring aside.

❷ Back

Use 20" (51cm) of thread to repeat Step 1,
but don't trim the thread. Weave through
beads to exit from an outside hole of 1C
added in Round 2.

❸ Join

Align the front and back of the beaded bead
so the C interlock, with the D and A facing
out. Use the working thread of the back to
*string 1A; pass through the outside hole of
the front's next C. String 1A; pass through
the outside hole of the back's next C. Repeat
from * seven times to completely connect
the front and back, adding a total of 16A
(FIG. 3). Weave through the beads again to
reinforce; secure the thread and trim. Set the
beaded bead aside.

❹ Assembly

Connect chain, wire, and a dangle to the
body to finish the earring:

DANGLE: Use 1 head pin to string 1 bead
cap (from outside to inside) and 1 melon
round; form a wrapped loop (FIG. 4). Set
aside.

LINK: Form a wrapped loop on one end of
one 2½" (6.5cm) piece of wire. String
the beaded bead, passing under the B
of Round 1 and through the openings
between the C of Round 2 on either the
front or the back; form a wrapped loop,
making sure the first and second loops of
the link face the same direction (FIG. 5).

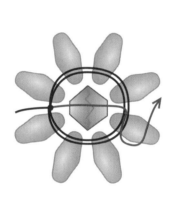

FIG. 1: Forming Round 1 and
adding the center of the front

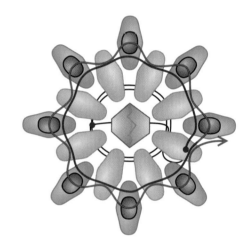

FIG. 2: Adding Rounds 2
and 3 of the front

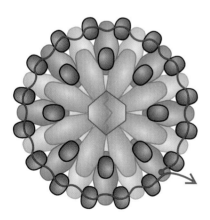

FIG. 3: Joining the front and back of the
beaded bead

FIG. 4: Forming the dangle

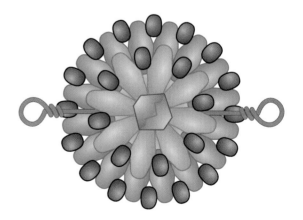

FIG. 5: Adding the wire to the beaded bead

TOP CHAINS: Use one 4mm jump ring to attach one end of the link to one end of one 1¼" (3.2cm) piece of chain; repeat using the other end of the link.

EAR WIRE: Use one 6mm jump ring to attach the free ends of the chains to an ear wire.

BOTTOM CHAINS: Use one 4mm jump ring to attach one end of the link to one end of one ¾" (2cm) piece of chain; repeat using the other end of the link.

DANGLE: Use one 6mm jump ring to attach the free ends of the chains to the dangle.

5 Repeat Steps 1–4 for a second earring.

Artist's Tips

- Barbara used Superduos for this project instead of their Twin counterparts because the tapered ends of the Superduos fit together much better than the slightly thicker ends of Twins.

- Use either shorter or longer lengths of chain to alter the finished length. Be sure that the wrapped loops on the side of the beads are positioned in the same direction (with the open loop facing the front).

- The beaded beads make great components for other projects. For example, stitch them together for a necklace or bracelet.

- If the beaded bead tips forward, try reinserting the wrapped loop slightly higher than center: Raising the center of gravity can prevent tipping. Also, you can use chain-nose pliers to "tweak" the wrapped loops slightly until the bead centers itself.

MAIN COLORWAY

Cathedral Windows

Jennifer and Susan Schwartzenberger

techniques

Tubular, circular, and flat peyote stitches

Fringe

materials

1 g bronze size 15° Japanese seed beads (A)

3 g bronze size 11° Japanese seed beads (B)

2 g bronze size 8° Japanese seed beads (C)

4 g crystal gold luster 5×2.5mm 2-hole SuperDuos (D)

28 tanzanite 4mm crystal bicones (E)

2 foil-back tanzanite 14mm crystal rivolis

2 bronze 4mm wireguards

1 pair of bronze 10×20mm ear wires

Taupe nylon beading thread

tools

Scissors

Size 11 or 12 beading needle

2 pairs of chain- or flat-nose pliers

FINISHED SIZE: 3" (7.5cm)

1 Bezel

Use tubular peyote stitch to form a bezel around the rivoli:

BEZEL ROUNDS 1 AND 2: Use 5' (1.5m) of thread to string 34B, leaving a 6" (15cm) tail. Use the working and tail threads to tie a knot, leaving a small space between the first and last beads strung to form a circle with relaxed tension. Pass through the first B strung (FIG. 1, PURPLE THREAD).

BEZEL ROUND 3: String 1B, skip 1B of the previous round, and pass through the following B; repeat sixteen times. *NOTE: Step up for this and subsequent rounds by passing through the first bead added in the current round unless otherwise noted* (FIG. 1, GREEN THREAD).

BEZEL ROUND 4: Work 17 stitches with 1A in each stitch (FIG. 1, BLUE THREAD).

BEZEL ROUND 5: Repeat Bezel Round 4. Repeat the thread path of this round. Weave through beads to exit from 1B of Bezel Round 1 (FIG. 1, RED THREAD). Insert 1 rivoli faceup into the beadwork; hold it in place while working the following rounds.

BEZEL ROUND 6: Work 17 stitches with 1A in each stitch (FIG. 2, BLUE THREAD).

BEZEL ROUND 7: Repeat Bezel Round 6. Weave through beads to exit from 1B of Bezel Round 2 (FIG. 2, RED THREAD).

2 Edge

Use circular peyote stitch to form an edge around the bezel:

EDGE ROUND 1: String 1B and pass through the next B of Bezel Round 2; repeat sixteen times (FIG. 3, PURPLE THREAD).

EDGE ROUND 2: Work 17 stitches with 1C in each stitch (FIG. 3, GREEN THREAD).

EDGE ROUND 3: Work 17 stitches with 1D in each stitch (FIG. 3, BLUE THREAD).

EDGE ROUND 4: String 1A and 1E; pass through the second (outside) hole of the next D in Edge Round 3. String 1E and pass through the next D (outside hole) of Edge Round 3; repeat ten times. String 1E and 1A; pass through the next D (inside hole) of Edge Round 3. Weave through beads to exit from the inside then outside holes of the last D exited in the previous round (FIG. 3, RED THREAD). *NOTE: You'll now begin working in the opposite direction.*

3 Bail

Use flat peyote stitch and fringe to create a bail that will form the top of the earring:

ROW 1: String 1D and pass through the next D (outside hole) of Edge Round 3; repeat three times. *NOTE: Step up for this and subsequent rows by passing through the outside hole of the last D added in the current row; each step up will change the stitching direction* (FIG. 4, PURPLE THREAD).

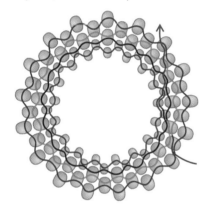

FIG. 1: Stitching Bezel Rounds 1–5

FIG. 2: Working Bezel Rounds 6 and 7

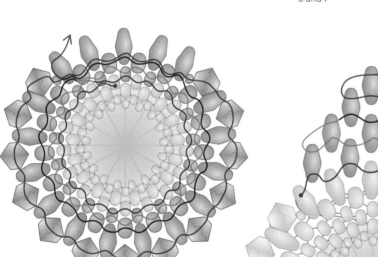

FIG. 3: Adding the edge

FIG. 4: Stitching Rows 1–4 of the bail

ROW 2: Work 3 stitches with 1D in each stitch, passing through the outside holes of the D in the previous row (FIG. 4, GREEN THREAD).

ROW 3: Work 2 stitches with 1D in each stitch (FIG. 4, BLUE THREAD).

ROW 4: Work 1 stitch with 1D (FIG. 4, RED THREAD).

EAR-WIRE LOOP: String 1A, 1B, 1A, 1E, 1A, 1 wireguard, and 1A; pass back through the E. String 1A, 1B, and 1A; pass through the last D (outside hole) exited (FIG. 5, BLUE THREAD). Repeat the thread path of the loop to reinforce. Weave back through all rows of the bail to reinforce the beadwork (FIG. 5, RED THREAD). Secure the threads and trim. Attach an ear wire to the loop of the wireguard by opening and closing the loop of the ear wire as you would a jump ring.

4 Repeat Steps 1–3 for a second earring.

Artist's Tips

- Your thread tension and bead choices can change the fit of the bezel. If you find the circle formed by Rounds 1–3 is too tight, remake it using two more beads in the starting circle because a rivoli will never sit evenly in a bezel that is too small. Adjust the bead counts in the following rounds accordingly. If needed, work additional rounds of size 15°s on the front and back to tighten the bezel and securely enclose the rivoli.

- Start with the size 11 beading needle, but switch to the size 12 if the bead holes fill up with thread too quickly. Don't force the needle through or you might break the bead.

- Before stringing a SuperDuo, make sure both holes are open; some special coatings can occasionally narrow or block the holes. If you find a closed or narrow hole in a SuperDuo already woven into your beadwork, use a fine-tip awl to gently ream the hole.

FIG. 5: Adding the ear-wire loop

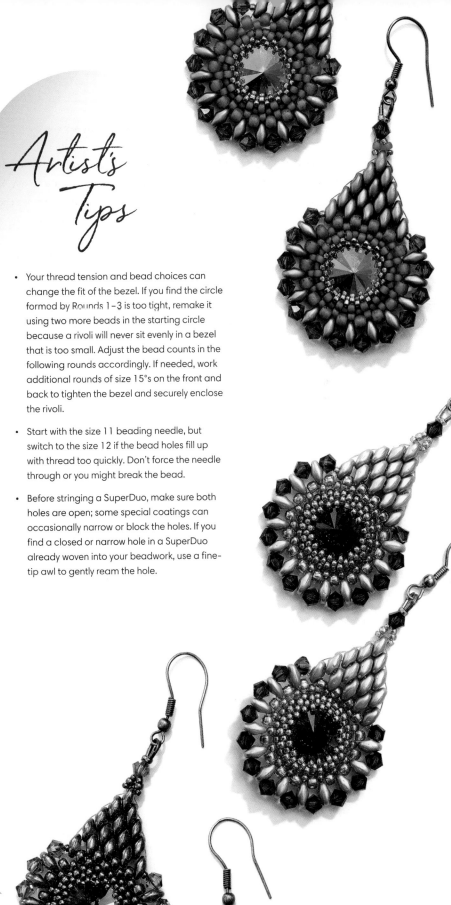

MAIN COLORWAY

Rising Phoenix

Penny Dixon

techniques

Cubic and tubular right-angle weave

Peyote stitch

Netting

Picot

materials

1 g bronze size 15° seed beads (A)

1 g matte iris teal size 15° seed beads (B)

2 g bronze size 11° seed beads (C)

1 g higher metallic violet luster size 11° seed beads (D)

1 g bronze size 8° seed beads (E)

1.5 g moondust turquoise 5×2.5mm 2-hole seed beads (F)

1 g bronze 3.4mm Japanese drops (G)

2 bronze 4mm fire-polished rounds (H)

8 opaque bronze smoke luster 6mm fire-polished rounds (J)

32 oxidized bronze 6mm flat 2-hole triangles (K)

1 pair of bronze 20mm ear wires

Smoke 6 lb braided beading thread

tools

Scissors

Size 12 beading needle

2 pairs of chain- or flat-nose pliers

FINISHED SIZE: 1⅝ × 2½" (4 × 6.5cm)

1 Center Component

Use netting and picots to form the center of the earring:

CENTER ROUND 1: Use 2' (6cm) of thread to string {1C and 1J} four times, leaving a 6" (15cm) tail. Use the working and tail threads to tie a knot, forming a tight circle. Pass through the first 1C/1J/1C (FIG. 1, BLUE THREAD).

CENTER ROUND 2: String 1E, 1G, and 1E, then pass through the last C exited in Center Round 1 and the next 1J/1C; repeat twice. String 1E, 1G, and 1E; pass through the last C exited in Center Round 1. Weave through beads to exit back through the first G of this round (FIG. 1, RED THREAD).

CENTER ROUND 3: String 2B, 1F, and 2B; pass through the last G exited. Weave through beads to exit back through the next G of Center Round 2. Repeat from the beginning of this round three times. Weave through beads to pass through the first (inside) hole of the first F in this round, then pass through the second (outside) hole of the current F (FIG. 2).

CENTER ROUND 4: String 1C and pass through the outside hole of the next F in Center Round 3; repeat three times. *NOTE: This will pull the F toward the center of the beadwork to sit on top of Center Round 1; the outside hole of each F now becomes an inside hole.* Pass through the first 1C/inside hole of 1F/1C/inside hole of 1F. Weave through beads to exit from the third G of Center Round 2 (FIG. 3, GREEN THREAD).

CENTER ROUND 5: String 1D, 1E, and 1D; pass through the last G exited and the next E of Center Round 2. String 6A; pass through the next 1E/1G of Center Round 2.* String 1B, 3G, and 1B; pass through the last G exited of Center Round 2 and the next E of Center Round 2. String 6A; pass through the next 1E/1G of Center Round 2. Repeat from the beginning of this round to * twice, but do not pass back through the 1G on the final repeat (FIG. 3, BLUE THREAD).

CENTER ROUND 6: Weave through beads to exit through the second G of Center Round 5. String 7A; pass through the last G exited. *NOTE: This forms the ear-wire loop.* Weave through beads to exit through the first E of Center Round 5 (FIG. 3, RED THREAD). Repeat the thread path to reinforce the A of Center Round 5 and the ear-wire loop. Secure the thread and trim.

2 Wing 1

Use cubic right-angle weave and peyote stitch to form a wing:

CUBE 1: Use 3' (91.5cm) of thread to string {1D and 1C} twice, leaving a 6" (15cm) tail; pass through first 3 beads again to form the first face of the cube. String 3C; pass through the last D exited and the first 2C just added for the second face. String 3C; pass through the last C exited and the first 2C just added for the third face (FIG. 4, BLUE THREAD). String 1C, pass through the end D of the first face, and string 1C; pass through the last C exited in the third face, the first C just added, and the first D of the first face (FIG. 4, RED THREAD).

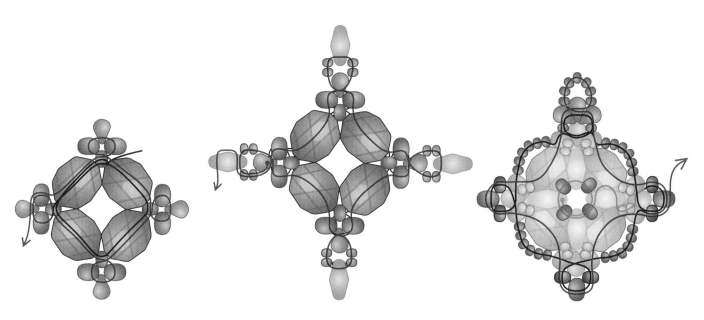

FIG. 1: Forming Center Rounds 1 and 2

FIG. 2: Stitching Center Round 3

FIG. 3: Working Center Rounds 4–6

CUBE 2, FACE 1: String 1C, 1D, and 1C; pass through the last D exited in the previous Cube and the first C just added (FIG. 5, ORANGE THREAD).

CUBE 2, FACE 2: String 2C; pass back through the next top C of the previous cube, up through the first side C of the previous face, and through the 2C just added and the next top C of the previous cube (FIG. 5, PURPLE THREAD).

CUBE 2, FACE 3: String 2C; pass through the nearest side C of Cube 2, Face 2. Pass through the last C exited in the previous cube and the first C just added (FIG. 5, GREEN THREAD).

CUBE 2, FACE 4: String 1C; pass down through the nearest side C of Cube 2, Face 1. Pass back through the next top C of the previous cube and up through the nearest side C of Cube 2, Face 3. Pass through the C just added (FIG. 5, BLUE THREAD).

CUBE 2, TOP: Pass through all the top beads of Faces 1–4; pull the thread tight to complete the cube. Pass through the top D of Cube 2, Face 1 again (FIG. 5, RED THREAD).

CUBES 3–6: Repeat Cube 2, Faces 1–4 and Cube 2, Top four times, using the top of the previous cube as the bottom of each new cube.

EMBELLISHMENT ROW 1: Turn the beadwork so Face 2 is faceup. Pass down through the nearest side C of Face 1 and through the bottom C of Face 2. String 1E and pass through the bottom C of the next cube; repeat four times. String 1E; pass up through the side C of Cube 1, Face 2 and through the top C of the same face (FIG. 6).

EMBELLISHMENT ROW 2: String 1K (left hole) and 2B, then pass through the top C of the next cube; repeat four times. Weave through beads to exit from the first E of the previous row, toward the center of the beadwork (FIG. 7, BLUE THREAD). *NOTE: Be sure the points of the K face outward when stringing.*

EMBELLISHMENT ROW 3: String 2B, then pass through the second hole of the nearest K and the next E of the previous row; repeat four times (FIG. 7, RED THREAD). Secure the threads, but do not trim the working thread. Trim the tail thread. Weave the working thread through beads to exit from the end D of Cube 1, away from the nearest K. Set aside.

③ Wing 2

Repeat Step 2, this time working Embellishment Rows 1–3 Face 4 instead of Face 2 of the cubes to form a wing that mirrors Wing 1.

Artist's Tip

- Keep tension tight when adding the two-hole triangle beads to create the bend in the wings.

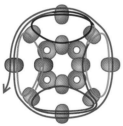

FIG. 4: Forming Cube 1 of Wing 1

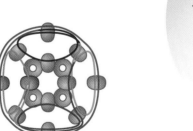

FIG. 5: Stitching Cube 2 of Wing 1

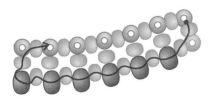

FIG. 6: Adding Embellishment Row 1 of Wing 1

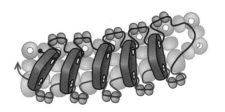

FIG. 7: Completing Embellishment Rows 2 and 3 of Wing 1

❹ Beaded Drop

Use netting and tubular right-angle weave to form a beaded drop:

DROP ROUND 1: Use 3' (91.5cm) of thread to string {1C and 1F} three times. Use the working and tail threads to tie a knot, forming a tight circle. Pass through the first 1C/1F (inside hole), then pass through the second (outside) hole of the current F (FIG. 8, GREEN THREAD).

DROP ROUND 2: String 1A, 1F, and 1A, then pass through the second (outside) hole of the next F in the previous round; repeat twice. Pass through the first 1A/1F (inside hole)/1A of this round (FIG. 8, BLUE THREAD).

FIG. 8: Beginning the beaded drop

DROP ROUND 3: String 5A and pass through next 1A/1F (inside hole)/1A of the previous round; repeat twice. Pass through the first 5A of this round and the next A of the previous round (FIG. 8, RED THREAD).

DROP ROUND 4: String 1A; pass through the nearest C of Drop Round 1. String 1A; pass through the next A of Drop Round 2, 5A of Drop Round 3, and A of Drop Round 2. Repeat from the beginning of this round twice. Weave through beads to exit from the first 3A of the next 5A in Drop Round 3 (FIG. 9, ORANGE THREAD).

DROP ROUND 5: String 1K (left hole) and pass through the outside hole of the next F in Drop Round 2. String 1K (left hole) and pass through the center A of the next 5A in Drop Round 3. Repeat from the beginning of this round twice. Weave through beads to exit from the second K of this round (inside hole), then pass through the second (outside) hole of the same K (FIG. 9, PURPLE THREAD). *NOTE: Be sure the points of the K face outward when stringing. You will now begin stitching in the opposite direction.*

DROP ROUND 6: String 1G and pass through the outside hole of the next K in the previous round; repeat five times (FIG. 9, GREEN THREAD).

DROP ROUND 7: String 1A, 1D, and 1A; pass through the outside hole of the last K exited and the first A just added. *String 1D and 1A; pass back through the outside hole of the next K in Drop Round 5, up through the nearest A of this round, and through the 1D/1A just added and the outside hole of the next K in Drop Round 5. String 1A and 1D; pass down through the nearest A of the previous unit, through the outside hole of the K just exited, and up through the A just added. Repeat from *. String 1D; pass down through the nearest A of this round, back through the outside hole of the nearest K in Drop Round 5, up through the last A of this round, and through the D just added (FIG. 9, BLUE THREAD).

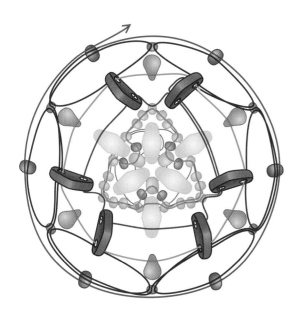

FIG. 9: Working Drop Rounds 4–8

FIG. 10: Assembling the earring

DROP ROUND 8: Pass through all the D of Drop Round 7; pull the thread tight (FIG. 9, RED THREAD). Weave through beads to exit from 1C of Drop Round 1. Secure the tail thread and trim; don't trim the working thread.

⑤ Assembly

Use netting to connect the wings and components:

CONNECTION 1: Use the working thread of Wing 1 to pass up through the leftmost E of the center component. String 1E and 1C; pass through the last D exited in Wing 1, the last E exited in the center component, and the 1E/1D just added. Repeat the thread path to reinforce (FIG. 10, ORANGE THREAD). Secure the thread and trim.

CONNECTION 2: Use the working thread of Wing 2 to repeat Connection 1, attaching the wing to the rightmost E of the center component (FIG. 10, PURPLE THREAD).

CONNECTION 3, STITCH 1: Use the working thread of the beaded drop to string 1A, 1D, 1H, 1D, and 1A; pass up through the end D on the free end of Wing 1, up through the 1D/1G/1D at the bottom of the center component, and down through the end D on the free end of Wing 2. String 1A; skip 1A and pass back down through the following 1D/1H/1D/1A of this stitch and through the last C exited in the beaded drop (FIG. 10, GREEN THREAD).

CONNECTION 3, STITCH 2: Pass through the top hole of the following F and through the next C. String 1A; pass up through the 1D/1H/1D/1A of Connection 3, Stitch 1 and the end D of Wing 1. Pass through the 1D/1G/1D at the bottom of the center component and down through the end D of Wing 2 and the following A of Connection 3, Stitch 1. Pass back down through the 1D/1H/1D of Connection 3, Stitch 1 and the A just added. Pass through the last C exited in the beaded drop, the top hole of the following F (not shown in FIG. 10 for clarity), and the next C (FIG. 10, BLUE THREAD).

CONNECTION 3, STITCH 3: Repeat Connection 3, Stitch 2, adding 1A and repeating the same thread path as Stitches 1 and 2 (FIG. 10, RED THREAD). Secure the thread and trim.

EAR WIRE: Attach an ear wire to the ear-wire loop by opening and closing the loop as you would a jump ring.

⑥ Repeat Steps 1–5 for a second earring.

MAIN COLORWAY

Four Corners

Michelle McEnroe

techniques

Circular peyote stitch

Netting

Picot

materials

2 g matte opaque olive-green size 15°
seed beads (A)

2 g silver-lined transparent light amethyst AB size 15°
seed beads (B)

2 g metallic bronze size 15° seed beads (C)

2 g metallic bronze size 11° seed beads (D)

2 g metallic plum size 11° seed beads (E)

2 g galvanized purple size 11° cylinder
beads (F)

40 opaque ultraluster green 5×2mm or 5×2.5mm 2-hole
seed beads (G)

2 New British Columbia jade 10mm rounds (H)

1 pair of gold-plated 1¼" (3.2cm) ear wires

Smoke 6 lb braided beading thread

tools

Size 12 beading needle

Scissors

2 pairs of chain- or flat-nose pliers

FINISHED SIZE: 1 ½ × 3" (3.8 × 7.5cm)

① Earring

Use circular peyote stitch and picots to form the body of an earring:

ROUND 1: Use 3' (91.5cm) of thread to string 1H, 5F, 1D, and 5F; pass through the H, leaving a 5" (12.5cm) tail (FIG. 1, GREEN THREAD). String 5F, 1D, and 5F; pass through the H and the original 5F/1D/5F added, allowing this strand of beads to wrap around the other side of the H (FIG. 1, BLUE THREAD). String 1D and pass through the next 5F/1D/5F; repeat. Pass through the nearest 1D and 2F (FIG. 1, RED THREAD).

ROUND 2: String 1A, 1C, and 1A; skip 1F of Round 1 and pass through the next 2F and 1D of Round 1 to form a picot. String 3D; pass through the last D exited and the next 2F of Round 1 to form a picot. Repeat from the beginning of the round three times. Pass through the nearest 2F (FIG. 2).

ROUND 3: String 2G, then skip 1F of Round 1 and pass through the next 2F and 1D of Round 1, the 3D picot of Round 2 to reinforce, and the next 2F of Round 1; repeat twice. String 2G; skip 1F of Round 1 and pass through the next 2F and 1D of Round 1 and the first 2D of the final Round 2 picot (FIG. 3, BLUE THREAD). *NOTE: Allow the 2G to lie behind the 1A/1C/1A picots of Round 2. You will now begin stitching in the opposite direction.*

ROUND 4: String 3A; pass through the outside hole of the next G of Round 3. String 2G; pass through the outside hole of the following G of Round 3. String 3A; pass through the center D of the next 3D picot of Round 2. Repeat from the beginning of the round three times. Weave through beads to exit from the inside hole of the first G added in this round (FIG. 3, RED THREAD).

ROUND 5: String 1G; pass through the inside hole of the next G added in Round 4, the nearest G of Round 3, and the next 3A of Round 4. String 3B; pass through the next 3A of Round 4 and the 2 nearest G. Repeat from the beginning of the round three times, exiting through the outside hole of the nearest G in Round 3 in the final repeat (FIG. 4).

ROUND 6: String 2A; pass through the outside hole of the nearest G in Round 4. String 2A; pass through the outside hole of the nearest G in Round 5. String 2A; pass through the outside hole of the next G in Round 4. String 2A; pass through the outside hole of the next G in Round 3. Weave through beads to exit from the outside hole of the next G in Round 3. Repeat from the beginning of the round three times. Weave through beads to exit from the fourth A added in this round (FIG. 5). Rotate the work so the thread exits the top of the beadwork.

ROUND 7: String 1C, 1E, and 1C; pass through the fifth and sixth A added in Round 6, the outside hole of the next 1G in Round 4, the nearest 2A, and the outside hole of the next G in Round 3. String 2A; pass through the inside hole of the nearest G in Round 3. String 1E; pass through the inside hole of the next G in Round 3. String 2A; pass through the outside hole of the last G exited and weave through beads to exit the first E added in this round (FIG. 6). Weave through beads to exit from the fourth A added in Round 6 on the next point; repeat this entire section three times. Weave through beads to exit from the first E added in this round.

LOOP: String 5E; pass through the last E exited, the next C, the outside hole of the nearest G in Round 5, the following C, and the next E to form a loop (FIG. 7, BLUE THREAD). String 1A and pass through the next E of the loop just formed; repeat five times. Weave through the C and G below as before, exiting the E (FIG. 7, RED THREAD). Repeat the thread path to reinforce.

EAR WIRE: Connect an ear wire to the loop just formed.

② Repeat Step 1 for a second earring.

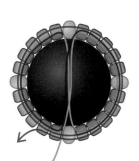

FIG. 1: Forming Round 1

FIG. 2: Adding Round 2

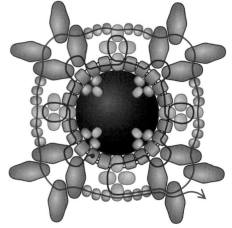

FIG. 3: Working Rounds 3 and 4

variation

This pattern also makes a very pretty pendant for a matching necklace or choker. Just connect a jump ring to the seed bead loop and then thread on a silk ribbon.

FIG. 4: Adding Round 5

FIG. 5: Stitching Round 6

FIG. 6: Working Round 7

FIG. 7: Adding the ear-wire loop

Champagne Serenade

Evelina Palmontová

techniques

Circular peyote stitch

Picot

materials

0.5 g antique bronze size 15° seed beads (A)

1.5 g bronze size 11° seed beads (B)

1 g starlight galvanized permanent-finish size 8° seed beads (C)

20 chalk champagne luster 5×3mm 2-hole Rullas (D)

6 chalk green pastel luster 6mm 2-hole diamond Silky beads (E)

16 crystal argent flare 3mm crystal bicones (F)

1 pair of stainless steel 12×18mm ear wires

Crystal 6 lb FireLine braided beading thread

tools

Scissors

Size 11 beading needle

FINISHED SIZE: 2⅞" (7.5cm)

MAIN COLORWAY

❶ Earring

Use circular peyote stitch and picots to form the earring body:

ROUND 1: *NOTE: Take care to string the E faceup.* Use 3' (91.5cm) of thread to string 1E and 1B, leaving a 4" (10cm) tail, then string {1D and 1B} five times (FIG. 1, PURPLE THREAD). String 1E and 1B, then string {1D and 1B} five times. Pass through the first (inside) hole of the first E in this round, the next B, and the first (inside) then second (outside) holes of the first D (FIG. 1, GREEN THREAD). *NOTE: You'll now begin working in the opposite direction.*

ROUND 2: String 1C and 2B, pass through the second (outside) hole of the nearest E, and string 2B. String 1C and pass through the following D (outside hole); repeat four times (FIG. 1, BLUE THREAD). Repeat from the beginning of this round. Pass through the first 1C/2B of this round (FIG. 1, RED THREAD).

ROUND 3: String 5B; pass through the next 2B/1C of the previous round. String 4A and pass through the next C of the previous round; repeat four times. Pass through the next 2B (FIG. 2, PURPLE THREAD). Repeat from the beginning of this round. Pass through the next 7B/1C/1D (outside then inside holes)/1B (FIG. 2, GREEN THREAD).

ROUND 4: String 3B, skip the E, and pass through the next B, then weave through beads to exit from the B before the next E (FIG. 2, BLUE THREAD); repeat. Pass through the first 2B of this round (FIG. 2, RED THREAD).

CENTER: String {1B and 1F} three times, then string 1B and pass through the mirror B of the previous round (FIG. 3, GREEN THREAD); repeat. Pass through the first 1B/1F/1B/1F of this round (FIG. 3, BLUE THREAD. String 1F and pass through the mirror F; repeat. Weave through beads to

exit from the center B of the second 5B set in Round 3 (FIG. 3, RED THREAD).

❷ Ear Wire

Add the ear wire to the body of the earring:

PASS 1: *NOTE: Take care to string the E faceup.* String 3B, 1E, and 3B; pass through the last B exited and the first 3B just added (FIG. 4, PURPLE THREAD).

PASS 2: String 4B; pass through the second (top) hole of the E. String 4B; pass through the first (bottom) hole of the E and the first 4B just added (FIG. 4, GREEN THREAD).

PASS 3: String 5B; pass through the next 4B set in Pass 2 and weave through all the B of this step, exiting from the third B just added (FIG. 4, BLUE THREAD).

EAR WIRE: *NOTE: Take care that the front of the ear wire faces the same direction as the front of the E.* String 3B, an ear wire, and 3B and pass through the last B exited (FIG. 4, RED THREAD); repeat the thread path to reinforce.

❸

Repeat Steps 1 and 2 for a second earring.

FIG. 1: Stitching Rounds 1 and 2

FIG. 2: Forming Rounds 3 and 4

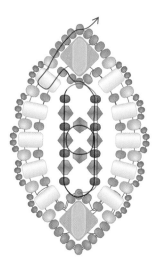

FIG. 3: Adding the center

FIG. 4: Attaching the ear wire

Tulip Mania

Reem Iversen

techniques
Tubular peyote stitch

Tubular herringbone stitch

Wireworking

materials
0.5 g metallic plum size 15° seed beads (A)

1 g metallic plum size 11° seed beads (B)

10 g blue iris 5×2.5mm 2-hole seed beads (C)

2 purple velvet 4mm crystal bicones

2 topaz AB 10×14mm faceted crystal teardrops

2 gold-plated 2" (5cm) head pins

2 gold-plated 18×24mm ear wires

Smoke 6 lb braided beading thread

Thread conditioner

tools
Scissors

Size 11 beading needle

Wire cutters

Flat-nose pliers

Round-nose pliers

FINISHED SIZE: 2⅜" (6cm)

1 Beaded Bead

Use tubular peyote stitch to form 2 domes, then zip them together to form a beaded bead:

TOP ROUND 1: Use 2' (61cm) of conditioned thread to string {1B and 1C} four times, leaving a 5" (12.5cm) tail; pass through all the beads again to a form a tight circle, then use the working and tail threads to tie a square knot. Pass through the first C strung and step up through the second (outer) hole of the same C (FIG. 1, GREEN THREAD). *NOTE: The stitching direction will change when you step up at the end of each round.*

TOP ROUND 2: String 2C and pass through the next C (outer hole) of Round 1; repeat three times. Pass through the first 2C added in this round, then step up through the outer hole of the second C (FIG. 1, RED THREAD). Pull the thread tight and hold the work so that it keeps its cup shape.

TOP ROUND 3: String 1C and pass through the next C (outer hole) of Round 2, then string 2C and pass through the following C (outer hole) of Round 2; repeat three times. Pass through the first C (inner hole) of this round and step up through the outer hole of the same C (FIG. 2, GREEN THREAD; shown flat for clarity).

TOP ROUND 4: String 1C and pass through the next C (outer hole) of Round 3; repeat eleven times. Secure the thread, but don't trim. Exit from the outer hole of the first C added in this round (FIG. 2, RED THREAD). Set the top dome aside.

BOTTOM: Repeat Top Rounds 1–3, leaving a 12" (30.5cm) tail. Secure and trim the working thread, but keep the tail thread intact.

ZIPPING: Place the top and bottom domes together so the beads interlock like a zipper. Use the working thread of the top dome to pass through the nearest 1C (outer hole) of Round 3 of the bottom dome, then pass through the next C (outer hole) of Round 4 of the top dome; repeat around to form a seamless beaded bead (FIG. 3). Repeat the thread path to reinforce. Secure the working thread and trim.

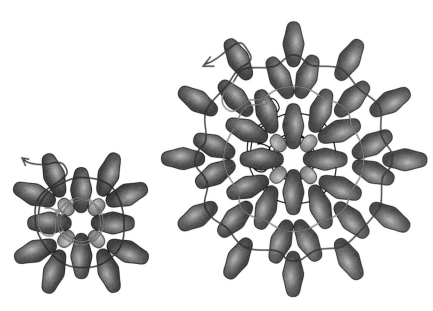

FIG. 1: Forming Rounds 1 and 2 of the top dome

FIG. 2: Stitching Rounds 3 and 4 of the top dome

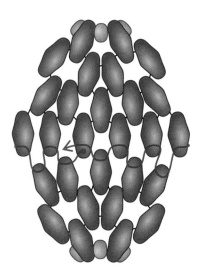

FIG. 3: Zipping the top and bottom domes together

2 End Cap

Work tubular herringbone stitch to form the earring's end cap:

CAP ROUND 1: Place a needle on the bottom dome's tail thread. Weave through beads to exit from a B of Bottom Round 1. String 2B and pass through the next B of Bottom Round 1; repeat three times (FIG. 4, ORANGE THREAD; shown flat for clarity). Step up through the first B added in this round. *NOTE: The B added in this round will sit on top of a C of Bottom Round 1.*

CAP ROUND 2: String 2B, pass down through the next B of Cap Round 1 and up through the following B; repeat three times. Step up through the first B of this round (FIG. 4, GREEN THREAD).

CAP ROUND 3: String 2B; pass down through the next B of Cap Round 2. String 1A; pass up through the following B of Cap Round 2, to form an increase. Repeat from the beginning of this round three times. Step up through the first B of this round (FIG. 4, BLUE THREAD).

CAP ROUND 4: String 1A; pass down through the next B of Cap Round 3. String 2A; pass up through the following B of Cap Round 3. Repeat from the beginning of this round three times (FIG. 4, RED THREAD). Repeat the thread path to reinforce. Secure the thread and trim.

3 Assembly

Use a head pin to string 1 teardrop (large end first), the beaded bead (end cap first), and one 4mm bicone; form a simple loop that connects to an ear wire.

4 Repeat Steps 1–3 for a second earring.

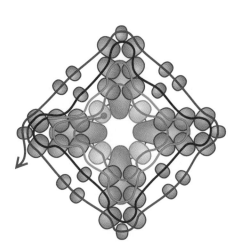

FIG. 4: Adding the end cap

- Keep thread tension tight throughout all rounds to encourage the beadwork to cup.

- If necessary to keep the work firm, pass through the beads of each round a second time, making half-hitch knots along the way. This will tighten and secure the thread.

MAIN COLORWAY

Arabesque

Debora Hodoyer

techniques

Right-angle weave variation

Circular peyote stitch variation

Picot

materials

0.5 g matte metallic antique silver size 15° seed beads (A)

0.5 g matte metallic antique silver size 11° seed beads (B)

2 opaque khaki AB 2.8mm drops (C)

12 white baby blue 2.5×3mm Minos par Puca beads (D)

4 pastel lime pearlescent 6mm 2-hole cabochons (E)

12 pastel Bordeaux 8×5mm 2-hole DiamonDuos (F)

4 white baby blue 10×5mm 3-hole Arcos par Puca beads (G)

1 pair of silver 10×20mm ear wires

Dark brown size D S-Lon beading thread

tools

Scissors

Size 12 beading needle

Chain-nose pliers

FINISHED SIZE: 1 × 2⅛" (2.5 × 5.3cm)

① Earring Body

Use a combination of stitches to form the earring body:

ROUND 1: Use 4' (122cm) of thread to string 1E (bottom hole, dome side up), 1B, 2F (top holes, faceted sides up), and 1B; pass through the E (bottom hole) to form a bottom loop, leaving a 5" (12.5cm) tail (FIG. 1, PURPLE THREAD). Repeat the thread path twice to secure. String 1B; pass through the top hole of the E (FIG. 1, GREEN THREAD). String 1B, 2F (bottom holes, faceted sides up), and 1B; pass through the top hole of the E to form a top loop (FIG. 1, BLUE THREAD). String 1B; pass through the bottom hole of the E and the 1B/2F/1B at the bottom of the E (FIG. 1, RED THREAD).

ROUND 2: String 1D and pass through next B of Round 1; repeat. Pass through the following 2F/1B. Repeat from the beginning of this round. Weave through beads to exit from the second D of this round (FIG. 2, GREEN THREAD).

ROUND 3: String 3B; pass through the nearest F (top hole). String 1F (right hole, faceted side up) and 5B; pass down through the same F (left hole) and the nearest F (top hole). String 3B; pass

down through the nearest 1D/1B (FIG. 2, BLUE THREAD). String 1G (top hole) and 5B; pass through the same 1G (bottom hole) and the nearest F (bottom hole). String 1F (left hole, faceted side up) and 5B; pass up through the same F (right hole) and the nearest F (bottom hole). String 1G (bottom hole) and 5B; pass through the same 1G (top hole) and the nearest B of Round 1. Weave through beads to exit up through the first 3B of this round (FIG. 2, RED THREAD).

ROUND 4: String 4A; pass through the nearest 5B of Round 3. String 4A; pass down through the next 3B of Round 3 and the nearest D (FIG. 3, PURPLE THREAD). String 5A; pass down through the next 5B of Round 3. String 3A and 1D; pass through the next 3B of Round 3 (FIG. 3, GREEN THREAD). String 3A, 1E (top hole, dome side up), and 3A; pass through the last B exited and the next 2B (FIG. 3, BLUE THREAD). String 1D and 3A; pass up through the next 5B of Round 3. String 5A; pass up through the nearest D of Round 2, then weave through all the beads of this round to exit from the first 3A added next to the E of this round (FIG. 3, RED THREAD).

DROP: String 3A; pass through the last E added (bottom hole). String 2B, 1C, and 2B; pass through the same E (bottom hole) to form a loop. String 3A; pass through the nearest 3A/1B/6A (FIG. 4, BLUE THREAD). String 1B; pass through the next 2B/1C/2B. String 1B; pass through the next 6A/1B/6A (FIG. 4, RED THREAD); repeat the thread path to reinforce. Weave through Round 4 beads to exit from the 1B at the center top of the earring.

LOOP: String 1B, 6A, and 1B; pass through the last B exited (FIG. 5). Repeat the thread path to reinforce. Secure the threads and trim.

② Ear Wire

Use chain-nose pliers to add an ear wire to the loop just formed.

③ Repeat Steps 1–2 for a second earring.

FIG. 1: Forming Round 1

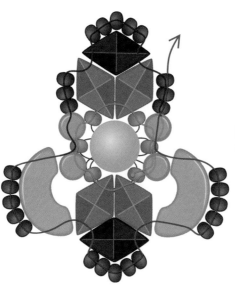

FIG. 2: Stitching Rounds 2 and 3

FIG. 3: Forming Round 4

FIG. 4: Adding the drop

FIG. 5: Stitching the loop

Artist's Tips

- Check to make sure there aren't any blocked holes in each of the two- and three-hole beads before stringing them. Discard any DiamonDuos or Arcos par Puca beads with blocked holes. Trying to unblock the holes can easily break these beads.

- Work with a moderate tension. If you pull the thread too much, the beadwork won't stay flat.

Beading Techniques

A few items of general information start off this section, followed by stitches, listed in alphabetical order.

Finishing and Starting Threads

Tie off the old thread when it's about 4" (10cm) long by making an overhand knot (see below) around previous threads between beads. Weave through a few beads to hide the knot, and trim the thread close to the work. Start the new thread by tying an overhand knot around previous threads between beads. Weave through several beads to hide the knot and to reach the place to resume beading.

Overhand Knot

This is the basic knot for tying off thread. Make a loop with the stringing material. Pass the cord that lies behind the loop over the front cord and through the loop; pull snug.

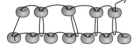

Pass Through vs Pass Back Through

Pass through means to move the needle in the same direction that the beads have been strung. Pass back through means to move the needle in the opposite direction.

Stop Bead

A stop bead (or tension bead) holds your work in place. To make one, string a bead larger than those you are working with, then pass through the bead one or more times, making sure not to split the thread.

Stepping Up

Use a step-up to prepare for the next row (or round). Unless otherwise directed, do this by exiting the first bead added in the current row/round.

Fringe

Exit from the foundation row of beads or fabric. String a length of beads plus 1 bead. Skipping the last bead, pass back through all the beads just strung to form a fringe leg. Pass back into the foundation row or fabric.

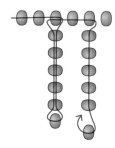

Herringbone Stitch

Form a foundation row of one- or two-needle even-count ladder stitch and exit up through the final bead. String 2 beads, pass down through the next bead in the ladder, and pass up through the following bead; repeat to the end of the row. Step up for the next row by wrapping the thread around previous threads to exit up through the last bead strung. To form the next row, string 2 beads and pass down through the second-to-last bead of the previous row and up through the following bead. Repeat, stringing 2 beads per stitch, passing down then up through 2 beads of the previous row and stepping up as before. The 2-bead stitch will cause the beads to angle in each column, like a herringbone fabric.

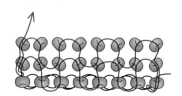

Brick Stitch

Stitch a foundation row in one- or two-needle ladder stitch. String 2 beads and pass under the closest exposed loop of the foundation row and back through the second bead. String 1 bead and pass under the next exposed loop and back through the bead just strung; repeat.

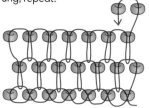

To decrease within a row, string 1 bead and skip a loop of thread on the previous row, passing under the second loop and back through the bead.

To increase within a row, work 2 stitches in the same loop on the previous row.

For **CIRCULAR BRICK STITCH,** work increases as needed to keep the work flat; at the end of each round, pass through the first and last beads to stitch them together, then string 2 beads to begin the next round.

For **TUBULAR BRICK STITCH,** join a ladder-stitched foundation row into a ring by passing through the first and last beads of the row, with the holes facing up. *String 1 bead and pass under the closest exposed loop of the foundation ring. Pass back through the same bead and repeat, adding 1 bead at a time. Finish the round by passing down through the first bead and up through the last bead of the current round, then string 2 beads to begin the next round.

Begin **TUBULAR HERRINGBONE STITCH** with a foundation ring of one- or two-needle even-count ladder stitch. String 2 beads. Pass down through the next bead and up through the following bead in the ladder. Repeat around the ring. At the end of the round, pass through the first beads of the previous and current rounds to step up to the new round.

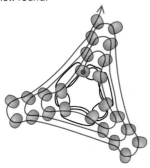

Ladder Stitch

For **ONE-NEEDLE LADDER STITCH,** string 2 beads and pass through them again. Manipulate the beads so their sides touch. String 1 bead. Pass through the last bead added and the bead just strung. Repeat, adding 1 bead at a time and working in a figure-eight pattern.

For **TWO-NEEDLE LADDER STITCH,** add a needle to each end of the thread. String 1 bead and slide it to the center of the thread. String 1 bead with one needle and pass the other needle back through the bead just added; repeat to form a strip.

Netting

String a base row of 13 beads. String 5 beads and pass back through the fifth bead from the end of the base row. String another 5 beads, skip 3 beads of the base row, and pass back through the next bead; repeat to the end of the row. To turn, pass back through the last 3 beads (one leg of the last net). String 5 beads, pass back through the center bead of the next net, and continue.

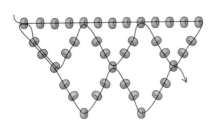

For **CIRCULAR NETTING,** string {1A and 1B} six times; pass through the beads again to form a circle for the foundation round and pass through the next 1A. *String 1A, 1B, and 1A; skip 1 bead and pass through the following bead in the previous round to form a "net." Repeat from * five times, then step up for the next round by passing through the first 2 beads of the first net. String 2A, 1B, and 2A; pass through the middle bead of the nearest net in the previous round. Repeat five times, then step up for the next round by passing through the first 3 beads of this round. Work each round the same way, increasing the number of A beads as necessary to keep the work flat, and stepping up by passing through the first half of the first net.

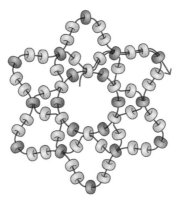

For **TUBULAR NETTING,** string {1A and 1B} six times; pass through the beads again to form the foundation round. *String 1A, 1B, and 1A; skip 1B and pass through the following 1B in the previous round to form a "net." Repeat from * twice, then step up for the next round by passing through the first 2 beads of this round. **String 1A, 1B, and 1A; pass through the middle bead of the nearest net in the previous round. Repeat from ** twice, then step up as before. Work each round the same way.

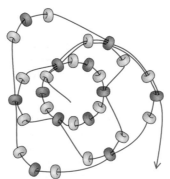

Peyote Stitch

For **ONE-DROP EVEN-COUNT FLAT PEYOTE STITCH,** string an even number of beads to create the first two rows. Begin the third row by stringing 1 bead and passing back through the second-to-last bead of the previous row. String another bead and pass back through the fourth-to-last bead of the previous row. Continue adding 1 bead at a time, passing over every other bead of the previous row.

TWO-DROP PEYOTE STITCH is worked the same as one-drop peyote stitch, but with 2 beads at a time instead of 1 bead.

For **ODD-COUNT FLAT PEYOTE STITCH,** string an uneven number of beads to create Rows 1 and 2. String 1 bead, skip the last bead strung, and pass through the next bead. Repeat across the row (this is Row 3). To add the last bead, string 1 bead and knot the tail and working threads, clicking all beads into place. Start the next row (Row 4) by passing back through the last bead added. Continue in peyote stitch, turning as for even-count at the end of this and all even-numbered rows. At the end of all odd-numbered rows, add the last bead, pass under the thread loop at the edge of the previous rows, and pass back through the last bead added.

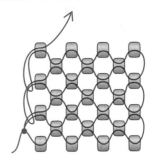

Begin a **MIDPROJECT PEYOTE-STITCH INCREASE** by working a stitch with 2 beads in one row. In the next row, work 1 bead in each stitch, splitting the pair of beads in the previous row. For a smooth increase, use very narrow beads for both the two-drop and the one-drop between.

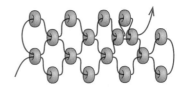

Odd-Count Flat Peyote Stitch End-Row Turnarounds

Working a strip of peyote stitch with an odd number of beads is a great choice when creating a motif that needs to come to a point or if you intend to attach something to the very center bead of the beadwork and you want symmetry. Here you'll see that there are several ways to work turnarounds at the end of the odd-number rows.

Start by stringing an odd number of beads. As with even-count peyote stitch, the first set of beads strung makes up both Rows 1 and 2. Note that the first bead strung remains the first bead of Row 1 (FIG. 1).

For Row 3, string 1 bead, skip the last bead previously added, and pass back through the next bead; repeat until you exit from the first bead of Row 2. Notice that this third row is worked just like even-count flat peyote until you reach the end (FIG. 2). To finish Row 3, string 1 bead and tie a square knot with the tail and working threads. Pass back through the last bead strung to step up for the next row (FIG. 3). For Row 4 and the following even-number rows, work across the row with 1 bead in each stitch (FIG. 4).

For Row 5 and the following odd-number rows, work across the row with 1 bead in each stitch until you exit the first bead of the previous row. Add the final bead of the row using one of the following methods.

Work odd-count peyote stitch when you want your embellishments to be perfectly centered.

Odd-count flat peyote stitch worked with the square-stitch add-on technique.

METHOD 1: TRADITIONAL (THREAD-LOOP) TURNAROUND

String 1 bead and pass the needle under the nearest thread loop at the end of the beadwork. Pass back through the last bead strung to step up for the next row. This is the most common way of working an odd-count turnaround (FIG. 5).

Alternate Rows 4 and 5 for the length of the work. The left edge of the beadwork will have odd-count turnarounds; the right edge will resemble even-count peyote stitch (FIG. 6).

METHOD 2: SQUARE-STITCH ADD-ON

Alternatively, you can finish odd-number rows with a square stitch. Before stringing the last bead of Row 3, pass back through the first bead of Row 1. String 1 bead, pass back through the first bead of Row 1 again, and pass through the bead just strung to complete the square stitch (FIG. 7). *NOTE: For subsequent odd-number rows, you'll add the final bead in the same manner.*

METHOD 3: CLOCKWISE FIGURE-EIGHT ADD-ON

Another way to add the last bead and step up for the next row is to work a figure-eight thread path in a clockwise direction. Before stringing the final bead of Row 3, pass back through the first bead of Row 1. String 1 bead, then pass back through the last bead exited in Row 2 and the next bead of Row 3 (FIG. 8, BLUE THREAD). Turn around by passing back through the second bead of Row 1, the next bead of Row 2, and the first bead of Row 1. Pass through the bead just added (FIG. 8, RED THREAD). *NOTE: For subsequent odd-number rows, you'll add the final bead in the same manner.*

METHOD 4: COUNTERCLOCKWISE FIGURE-EIGHT ADD-ON

When using the figure-eight method, you can also add the last bead with a counterclockwise thread path. String 1 bead, then pass through the first bead of Row 1, the nearest bead of Row 2, and the next bead of Row 1 (FIG. 9, BLUE THREAD). Turn around by passing through the second-to-last bead of Row 3, back through the nearest bead of Row 2, and back through the first bead of Row 1. Pass through the bead just added (FIG. 9, RED THREAD). *NOTE: For subsequent odd-number rows, you'll add the final bead in the same manner.*

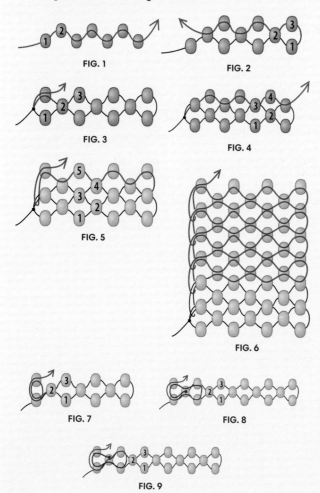

FIG. 1

FIG. 2

FIG. 3

FIG. 4

FIG. 5

FIG. 6

FIG. 7

FIG. 8

FIG. 9

To make a **MIDPROJECT PEYOTE-STITCH DECISION**, simply pass the thread through 2 beads without adding a bead in the "gap." In the next row, work a regular one-drop peyote stitch over the decrease. Work with tight tension to avoid holes.

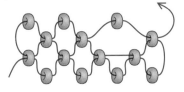

For **CIRCULAR PEYOTE STITCH,** string 3 beads and knot the tail and working threads to form the first round; pass through the first bead strung. For the second round, string 2 beads and pass through the next bead of the previous round; repeat twice. To step up to the third round, pass through the first bead of the current round. For the third round, string 1 bead and pass through the next bead of the previous round; repeat around, then step up at the end of the round. Continue in this manner, alternating the two previous rounds. It may be necessary to adjust the bead count, depending on the relative size of the beads, to keep the circle flat.

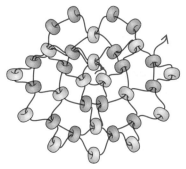

For **EVEN-COUNT TUBULAR PEYOTE STITCH,** string an even number of beads and knot the tail and working threads to form the first 2 rounds; pass through the first 2 beads strung. To work Round 3, string 1 bead, skip 1 bead, and pass through the next bead; repeat around until you have added half the number of beads in the first round. Step up through the first bead added in this round. For the following rounds, string 1 bead and pass through the next bead of the previous round; repeat, stepping up at the end of each round.

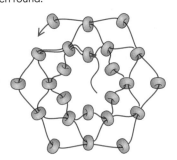

Work **ODD-COUNT TUBULAR PEYOTE STITCH** much the same as even-count tubular peyote stitch; however, it isn't necessary to step up at the end of each round.

Picot

A picot is a decorative net, most often made with 3 beads, used to embellish a beadwork surface. In the illustration, the small beads constitute the picot, which has been added to the edge of some beadwork.

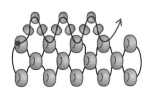

Right-Angle Weave

For **ONE-NEEDLE RIGHT-ANGLE WEAVE,** string 4 beads and pass through the first 3 beads again to form the first unit. For the rest of the row, string 3 beads and pass through the last bead exited in the previous unit and the first 2 beads just strung; the thread path will resemble a series of figure eights, alternating direction with each unit. To begin the next row, pass through beads to exit from the top bead of the last unit. String 3 beads and pass through the last bead exited and the first bead just strung. *String 2 beads; pass back through the next top bead of the previous row, the last bead exited in the previous unit, and the 2 beads just strung. Pass through the next top bead of the previous row. String 2 beads; pass through the last bead of the previous unit, the top bead just exited, and the first bead just strung. Repeat from * to complete the row, then begin a new row as before.

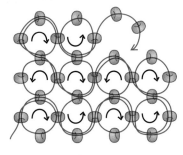

To begin **TWO-NEEDLE RIGHT-ANGLE WEAVE,** add a needle to each end of the thread. Use one needle to string 3 beads and slide them to the center of the thread. *Use one needle to string 1 bead, then pass the other needle back through it. String 1 bead on each needle, then repeat from * to form a chain of right-angle-weave units. To turn at the end of the row, use the left needle to string 3 beads, then cross the right needle back through the last bead strung. Use the left needle to string 3 beads, then cross the right needle back through the last bead strung. To continue the row, use the right needle to string 2 beads; pass the left needle through the next bead on the previous row and back through the last bead strung.

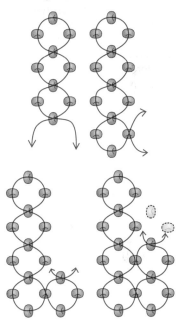

For **CUBIC RIGHT-ANGLE WEAVE,** string 4 beads, leaving a 3" (7.5cm) tail. Pass through the beads again to form a tight circle; use the working and tail threads to tie a square knot and pass through the first bead strung. For the first face of the cube, string 3 beads and pass through the last bead exited at the bottom of the cube, then pass through the first bead just added. For the second face of the cube, string 2 beads and pass back through the next bead at the bottom of the cube, then pass up through the nearest bead on the side of the first face, pass through the 2 beads just added, and pass through the next bead at the bottom of the cube. For the third face of the cube, string 2 beads; pass down through the nearest side bead on face 2, pass through the next bead at the bottom of the cube, and pass up through the first bead just added. For the fourth face of the cube, string 1 bead; pass down through the nearest side bead on face 1, pass back through the next bead at the bottom of the cube, pass up through the nearest side bead of face 3, and pass through the first bead just added. Pass through the 4 beads at the top to complete the cube. For subsequent cubes, the beads at the top of the previous cube will act as the bottom of the new cube.

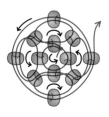

Square Stitch

String a row of beads. For the second row, string 2 beads; pass through the second-to-last bead of the first row and through the second bead just strung. Continue by stringing 1 bead, passing through the third-to-last bead of the first row, and passing through the bead just strung. Repeat this looping technique to the end of the row.

For **CIRCULAR SQUARE STITCH,** string the

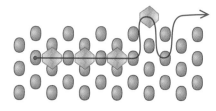

first round of beads and pass through them again to form a circle. Start a new round by stringing 2 beads; pass through the last bead of the first round and through the 2 beads just strung. Repeat around, passing through the next bead of the previous round for each 2 new beads strung. At the end of the round, pass through the whole round again to tighten the beads. Start a new round by stringing 2 beads; pass through the last bead of the previous round and through the 2 beads just strung. String 1 bead and pass through the next bead of the previous round and the bead just strung. Repeat around, stitching 1 or 2 beads to each bead of the previous round, adjusting the count as necessary to keep the work flat.

For **TUBULAR SQUARE STITCH,** string the first round of beads and pass through them again to form a circle. Start a new round by stringing 1 bead; pass through the last bead of the first round and through the bead just strung. Repeat around, passing through the next bead of the previous round for each new bead strung. At the end of the round, pass through the whole round again to tighten the beads.

Stitching in the Ditch

Layers of decoration can be easily added to previously stitched rows/rounds of beadwork. Exit one bead in the row/round you wish to embellish, string one decorative bead and pass through the next bead in the same row/round. Repeat as desired.

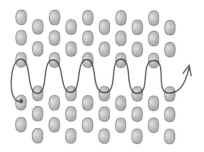

Zipping (aka Zipping Up)

This technique interlocks two edges of peyote stitch together like a zipper. Zip by passing the thread from an up bead on one edge of beadwork (indicated with a 1 in figure 000) to the up bead on the other edge of beadwork (2).

Wirework Techniques

Straightening Beading Wire

If your beading wire stays coiled and won't relax after being unspooled, place a weight on one end of the cord, unfurl the wire, and suspend the spool so the beading wire has time to relax—overnight or longer, if possible.

Head Pins/Eye Pins

Head pins are straight wires with a flat disc, ball, or other shape at one end. Eye pins are straight wires that end in a loop.

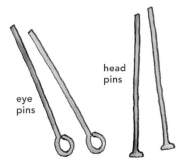

eye pins

head pins

Jump Rings

Jump rings connect holes and loops. Open a jump ring by grasping each side of its opening with a pair of pliers. Don't pull apart; instead, twist in opposite directions so that you can open and close without distorting the shape.

Simple Loops

Use flat-nose pliers to make a 90° bend at least ½" (1.3cm) from the end of the wire. Use round-nose pliers to grasp the wire at the tip; roll the pliers toward the bend, but not past it, to preserve the 90° bend. Adjust the pliers as needed to continue the wrap around the nose of the pliers. Trim the wire next to the bend.

Creating a perfectly round and centered simple loop takes practice. When you grip the tip/end of the wire with the round-nose pliers, place the tip of your nondominant thumbnail into the angled bend, and press your nondominant forefinger and thumb together and upward against the angled bend while you rotate your dominant wrist away from your body to form the loop. This combined action will help keep the angle sharp and the loop circular.

Open a simple loop by grasping each side of its opening with a pair of pliers. Don't pull apart. Instead, twist in opposite directions so that you can open and close it without distorting the loop's shape.

Wrapped Loops

Begin by making a 90° bend at least 2" (5cm) from the end of the wire. Use round-nose pliers to form a simple loop with a tail overlapping the bend. Wrap the tail tightly down the neck of the wire two or three times. Trim the excess wire to finish. Make a thicker, heavier-looking wrapped loop by wrapping the wire back up over the coils, toward the loop, and trimming at the loop.

Former *Beadwork* editor Debbie Blair has this tip for finishing wrapped loops: Use the rounded, football-shaped hole in the tip of crimping pliers to round out the end of the wire after forming a wrapped loop so the wire lays flat and doesn't poke out.

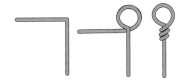

Making Ear Wires

Making ear wires lets you personalize your earrings right down to the hanging mechanism. You can use any wire you like—but factor in any metal allergies.

BASIC EAR WIRES: Cut 1½" (3.8cm) of wire and make a small loop at one end (FIGURE 1). Hold the loop against a marker (or any rod with a ½" [1.3cm] diameter, including a dowel) and bend the wire over the marker, away from the loop (FIGURE 2). Using round-nose pliers, make a small, outward bend at the end of the wire (FIGURE 3).

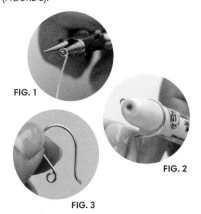

FIG. 1

FIG. 2

FIG. 3

SPIRALED EAR WIRES: Cut 1¾" (4.5cm) of wire and form a spiral at one end of it (FIGURE 1). Hold the spiral flat in a pair of chain-nose pliers and bend the wire perpendicular to the spiral (FIGURE 2). Hold the spiral against a marker (or a dowel with a ½" [1.3cm] diameter) and bend the wire over the marker, away from the spiral (FIGURE 3). Pinch the spiral against the finished ear wire (FIGURE 4).

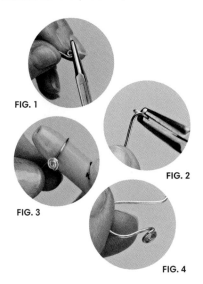

FIG. 1

FIG. 2

FIG. 3

FIG. 4

FLATTENED EAR WIRES: Ideally, you'll have a ball-peen hammer and a steel bench block to make these—but you can always make do with other tools. Cut 1¾" (4.4cm) of wire and hammer one tip flat on the bench block (FIG. 1). Bend the flattened tip up with round-nose pliers (FIG. 2). Hold the loop against a marker (or a dowel with a ½" [1.3cm] diameter) and bend the wire over the marker away from the loop (FIG. 3).

BALLED EAR WIRES: You'll need a torch to make these. Cut 1¾" (4.4cm) of copper, sterling, or fine silver wire. Holding it with pliers, ball up one end (FIG. 1), then cool it by quenching it in water. Using round-nose pliers, make a small loop at the balled end (FIG. 2). Hold the loop against a marker (or a dowel with a ½" [1.3cm] diameter) and bend the wire over the marker away from the loop (FIG. 3).

Cutting Chain

To cut a specific length of chain, measure it from one end, hold the link that's right at that measurement, and cut the *next* link.

To get multiple pieces of chain that are all exactly the same length, you only need to measure once, as follows. Measure and cut just one piece. Count the number of links in it, then for the remaining pieces of chain simply cut pieces with the same number of links.

Keeping Metal Tarnish-Free

Place antitarnish strips, along with your sterling silver metal (and any other metals that are affected by exposure to the atmosphere), inside zip-top bags. The antitarnish strips will help absorb the sulfides in the air trapped inside the bag, and the zip top will help prevent more oxygen (carrier of the sulfides) and moisture from entering the bag, thus protecting your metal from tarnish.

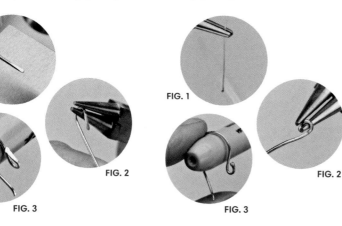

FIG. 1 FIG. 2 FIG. 3

FIG. 1 FIG. 2 FIG. 3

ball-peen hammer

steel bench block

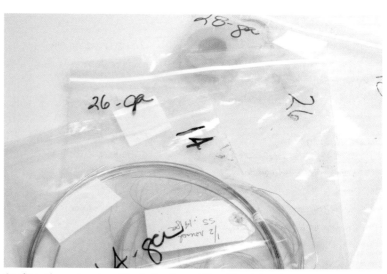

Sterling silver wire stored in zip-top bag with antitarnish strips.

Contributors

SANDIE BACHAND

MELINDA BARTA

ROBIJO BURZYNSKI
robijo@beadstitcher.com
www.beadstitcher.com

SONIA CORBIN-DAVIS
sonia.thejewelryinstructor@gmail.com
www.thejewelryinstructor.etsy.com

CSILLA CSIRMAZ

PENNY DIXON
pendixon@gmail.com
www.pennydixondesigns.com

CHERYL ERICKSON
cheryl@artisticbead.com
www.artisticbead.com

BARBARA FALKOWITZ
info@artfulbeadstudio.com
www.artfulbeadstudio.com

BREANNA GARCIA
www.astervelajewelry.etsy.com

CECILIA GUASTAFERRO
www.thebeadingplace.com

AMY HAFTKOWYCZ
info@artfulbeadstudio.com
www.artfulbeadstudio.com

TINA HAUER
www.ib-beading.com

DEBORA HODOYER
www.crownofstones.etsy.com

REEM IVERSEN
2BeadsR1@gmail.com

LISA KAN
www.lisakan.com
www.ariadesignstudio.com

ALICE KHARON
alice.kharon@yahoo.com

LUCY JOAN KING
lucyjoanking@hotmail.com
www.lucyjoandesigns.etsy.com

MICHELLE McENROE
glasscat@optonline.net

LINDA McKEE

MAGGIE MEISTER
www.mmmbeads.com

SUE A. NEEL
www.facebook.com/arcabeadies

CHRISTINA NEIT
www.goodquillhunting.com

EVELÍNA PALMONTOVÁ
www.svetrucnychprac.sk

BARBARA RICHARD

KASSIE SHAW
www.beadingbutterfly.com

JENNIFER and SUSAN
SCHWARTZENBERGER
paintcreekbeaddesign@yahoo.com
paintcreekbeaddesign.etsy.com

MELISSA GRAKOWSKY SHIPPEE
www.mgsdesigns.net

MONICA VINCI
www.loscrignodeigioielli.blogspot.it

AGNIESZKA WATTS (formerly Dutka)
www.agnesse.weebly.com

KRISTEN WINTER
www.wearwoofgallery.com

JILL WISEMAN
jill@tapestrybeads.com

Metric Conversion Chart		
To Convert	To	Multiply By
Inches	Centimeters	2.54
Centimeters	Inches	0.4
Feet	Centimeters	30.5
Centimeters	Feet	0.03
Yards	Meters	0.9
Meters	Yards	1.1

Explore the Beautiful Craft of
Handmade Jewelry!

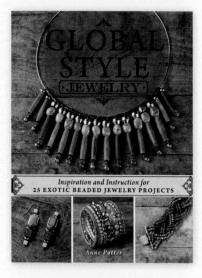

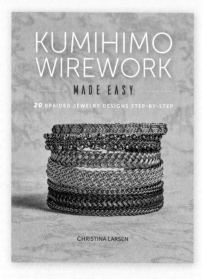

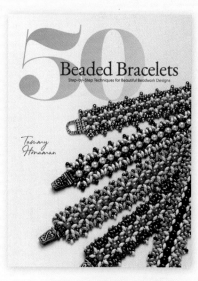

Global Style Jewelry

Inspiration and Instruction for 25 Exotic
Beaded Jewelry Projects

Anne Potter

978-1-63250-391-6
$22.99

Kumihimo Wirework Made Easy

20 Braided Jewelry Designs
Step-by-Step

Christina Larsen

978-1-63250-635-1
$24.99

50 Beaded Bracelets

Step-by-Step Techniques for Beautiful
Beadwork Designs

Tammy Honaman

978-1-63250-675-7
$24.99